The COMPLETE BOOK OF KARATE WEAPONS

THE COMPLETE BOOK OF KARATE WEAPONS

Dr. Theodore Gambordella

PALADIN PRESS
BOULDER, COLORADO

Also by Dr. Theodore Gambordella:

Fight for Your Life!
   The Secrets of Street Fighting

The 100 Deadliest Karate Moves

The Complete Book of Karate Weapons
by Dr. Theodore Gambordella

Copyright © 1991 by Dr. Theodore Gambordella

ISBN 0-87364-629-0
Printed in the United States of America

Published by Paladin Press, a division of
Paladin Enterprises, Inc., P.O. Box 1307,
Boulder, Colorado 80306, USA.
(303) 443-7250

Direct inquires and/or orders to the above address.

Dedication

To Keith Yates, Jim Toney, Barry Guimbellot, Steve Weiss, Russ Comerski, and Steve Rich, without whom this book would never have been written.

PHOTOS BY STEVE RICH

Contents

Introduction

I began my training in the martial arts over fourteen years ago in the little town of Alexandria, Louisiana. From the first I was interested in weapons, but I had great difficulty in finding any but a handful of people who knew anything about weapons. For many years I was only able to acquire little bits of weapons training from various teachers here and there. I tried to learn all that I could from books, but found that the number of books on weapons is almost as short in supply as the number of instructors with a knowledge of weapons. I also found that most of the books about weapons were written by the same man and were incomplete in their depth, for no books were available on the tonfa or the yawara, and only a few were available on the staff, the bo, and the knife. There seemed to be numerous books on the nunchaku, most poorly done, and a few books on the sai; but all in all the books available for the martial art student who was interested in weapons were few and far between.

So I decided to write my own book. I spent the last four years doing research and training with weapons, learning their use and applications. I was able to achieve a fourth degree black belt in weapons (kubojitsu), I had already written four other books and a movie script, "The Leopard," so I was familiar with what was necessary to write a good book. I wanted my book to have techniques that a beginner could learn, but that a teacher could also benefit from. I wanted to make the book easy to follow by avoiding any overuse of photos or confusing text. I wanted to include a basic practice Kata for each weapon, as well as techniques for the weapon's offensive and defensive use. Finally, I wanted to write a book that would serve as a manual on weapons for years to come—a book that a student or a teacher would be proud to own and would refer to whenever they had a question on weapons or wanted a new technique.

I feel that I have accomplished all of these goals in this book, *The Complete Book of Karate Weapons.* It is a book that I am proud of and one that you can be proud to have in your library. If you will read this book with an open mind and follow the techniques and exercises described herein, you can make yourself one of the few experts with weapons in the world today.

I could never have written this book without the help of many friends and fellow martial artists who appear with me in the instructional photos, both as technique partners and technical advisers. These men, some of the most outstanding black belts in the South, include:

Keith Yates: fourth degree black belt. Winner of many kata championships and weapons kata championships at the top tournaments of the South. A master artist who also designed the cover of the book.

James Toney: fifth degree black belt. Teacher extraordinaire and tournament champion for many years. One of the most respected teachers in Texas.

Barry Guimbellot: third degree black belt. Probably the most successful teacher in Dallas, an outstanding example of character and leadership in karate.

Steve Weiss: second degree black belt. A modern jiu-jitsu expert who is also an expert in karate.

1

Ross Comerski: first degree black belt. A giant of a man and a giant of a teacher.

Finally, I must thank all of my teachers through my years of training for their help and knowledge, such great men as: Soke R. Sacharnoski, Soke A. Church, Soke K. Marx, Master HeYoung Kimm, Shihan B. Pearson, Dr. J. Marler, and Sensi B. Hathorn. These great men and excellent teachers gave the knowledge and training that enabled me to get to where I am today. I am forever grateful to them and their arts.

Last, let me take a moment to thank the most important force in my life, my Lord and Savior, Jesus Christ, Who gives me the strength and ability necessary to write this book and to share my knowledge with my fellow martial artists.

Chapter 1

The Knife

The knife is probably the most common weapon in the world today, because it also serves as a tool for eating and work. It has been used by men from ancient times for defense and attack and still remains the favorite weapon of defense today.

The karate knife is a little different from a regular knife because of its construction. There should be a blade guard for protecting the hand of the user from the blade, as well as for gripping purposes, and a finger spot which the little finger wraps around when holding the knife for defense. This finger spot is on the blade, but is smooth and will not cut the hand. The handle should be very hard, for it is also used for striking, and the blade should be double bladed at the end, for cutting and slashing forward or backwards, but not double all the way down, for the protection of the user and for blocks.

The knife is the most dangerous weapon available for the beginner, because it is not just effective for defense, but can kill you when practicing if you handle it sloppily or carelessly. Therefore, I suggest that you practice your techniques with a rubber knife until such time as you are very proficient and a margin of safety is assured. Never joke with the knife or be foolish. The knife is a deadly weapon and must always be treated with respect.

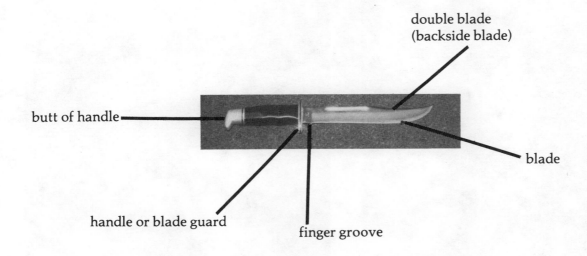

double blade (backside blade)

butt of handle

blade

handle or blade guard

finger groove

Holding Positions

The basic grip: hold the knife in the hand with the little finger wrapped around the guard and in the finger groove provided there.

Now wrap the rest of the fingers around the handle and extend the thumb down the top with the forefinger down to the end of the handle.

The blade should be pointed down and extended flat against the side of the forearm.

Side view.

Front view.

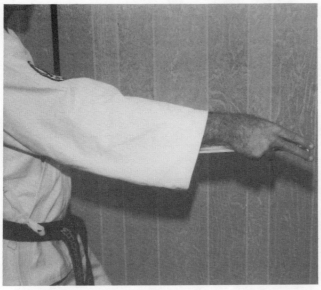

The knife can be held like this and concealed almost completely by using one or two fingers down the handle (for this photo I have let a little of the blade show so that you can get an idea of how I am holding the knife).

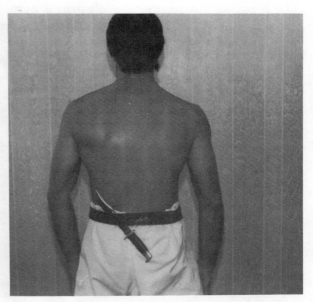

To carry the knife behind you, place it in your belt with the blade pointed down and the handle under the belt.

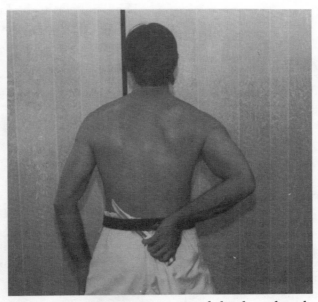

This makes it very easy to reach back and grab the knife for use.

Basic Stance

The modified cat stance: the left arm is across the body to block and to hide the knife while the right hand holds the knife.

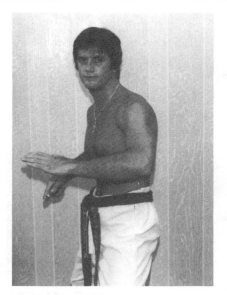

The front thrust: the knife is thrusted straight out in front of the body. Used for striking the eyes, stomach, groin, and throat.

The front slash: the knife is held with the blade out and slashes across the body. Used to cut the face, chest, back, legs, and arms.

The overhead stab: this is a power stabbing position. The blade should be pointed up and the thumb on the back of the handle for support.

The side slash (backhanded): the knife is held so that it extends out the side of the hand. Used for slashing the body. The palm is facing down, and the wrist is moving in a backhand motion.

The forehand slash: the palm faces up here, and the wrist moves in a forehand motion. Used for slashing faces and body parts.

The groin stab or underarm stab: the knife is held with the palm facing up and out to the right. Used for stabbing the back, groin, and abdomen.

The front thrust: the knife is held straight down the arm, and the forefinger goes down the side of the blade for thrusting accuracy. Used for thrusting into the eyes, throat, and groin.

The overhead stab: the knife is held with the blade pointing up and the wrist in the hand-shaking position. Used to stab the head and back.

The Throat Slash Using the Wrist Flick

This is an excellent and dangerous move that allows the knife to remain hidden to the last moment.

Begin by holding the knife concealed down your right forearm.

Now punch straight out with the hand as you would in a normal punch.

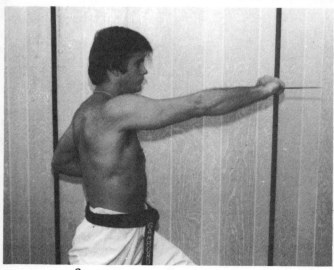

At the last second, flip the wrist very hard to the left and this will cause the blade of the knife to come around and out, for slashing the throat or eyes.

Throwing the Knife

There are several different methods used for throwing the knife, but the most practical one is to use an overhand throwing motion with the knife and let it flip over and then go into the target area.

Hold the knife so that it is balanced on your forefinger; this is the point at which the knife can be controlled most easily. A good knife should be balanced properly.

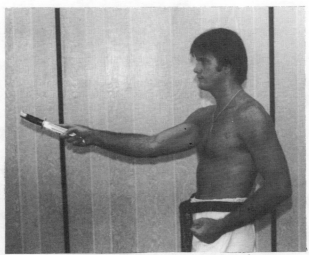

Now throw the knife in an overhand motion, just like you were throwing a ball.

With much practice you will be able to hit a very small target.

Striking Areas

Slashing the throat: the knife is held so that the blade is away from the body and you draw the blade across the throat, cutting it open.

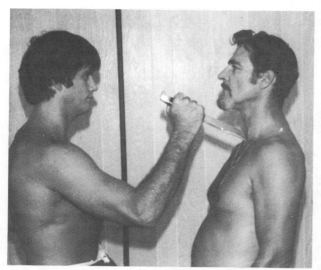

Stabbing the throat: thrust the end of the knife into the soft part of the throat.

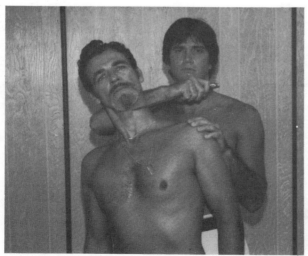

Take the point of the knife and stab it through the larynx, and then tear it out the front of the throat.

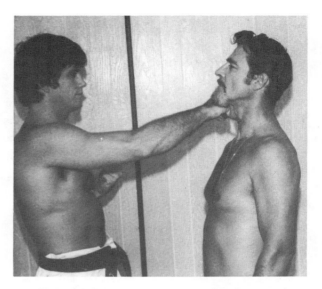

Cutting the throat from behind: take the blade of the knife and draw it across and down the throat.

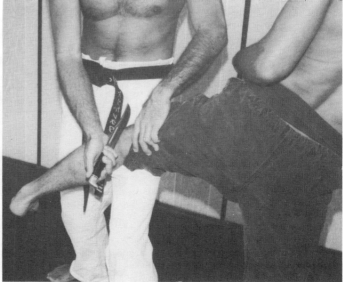

Slash the ligaments of the knee, or muscles of the calf with the knife.

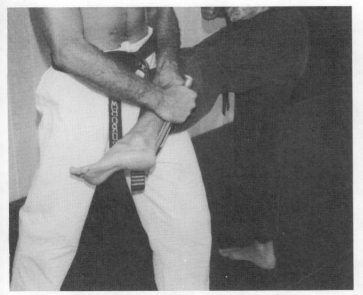

Cut the achilles tendon with the knife.

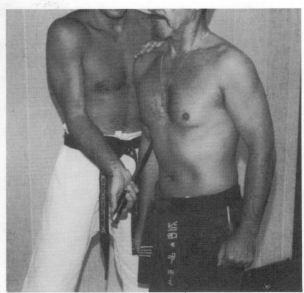

Stab the knife into the lungs and up into the heart.

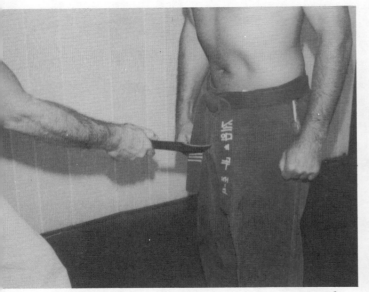

Stab the knife into the groin or lower stomach.

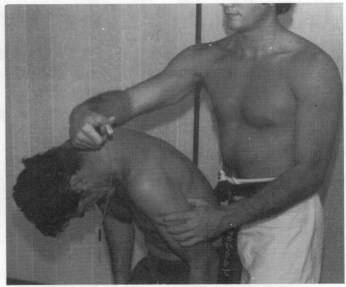

Cut the spinal cord and back of the neck with the knife.

Stab the kidneys.

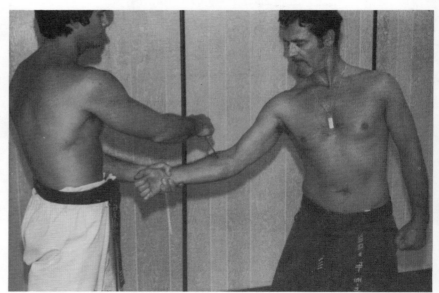

Cut the forearm muscles and bicep.

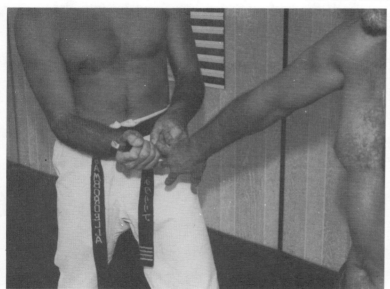

Slice open the web area between the fingers.

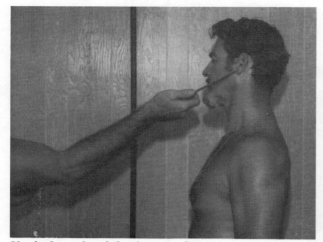

Slash the side of the face or throat.

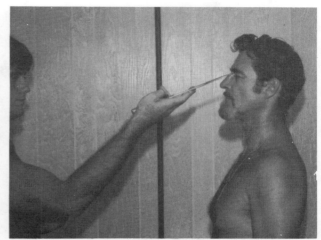

Poke the point into the eyes.

Techniques for Using a Knife Against an Unarmed Attacker

Special Note: I do not feel that there would *ever* be any need to use a knife against an unarmed attacker and do not advise or suggest you ever do so for any reason. These techniques are here to show karate techniques of defense using a knife and no further implications should be inferred or are intended.

Prepare for the attack.

Block the strike with the left arm and counter with a slash of the throat.

Finish with a stab into the back.

Prepare for the attack.

Block the punch with your left, and slash across the muscles of his forearm with the knife.

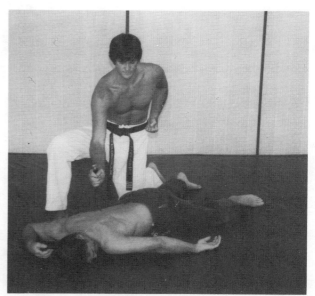

Finish him by coming over and slashing open the throat, then stabbing his back.

Block the punch by a middle block with your right arm, and then flip the knife over and cut open the wrist.

Now step in and thrust the knife into his abdomen.

Finish him by stabbing down into his throat.

Ready for the attack.

As he punches, block with your left and step up and thrust the knife into his throat.

15

Ready to block and counter.

Block the kick with the left forearm and cut the leg open with the knife in the right hand. Now spin to your right and come back with a backward thrust into his abdomen.

Come up and slash the knife across the face, then finish him by stabbing his back.

Ready for the attack. You counter but he grabs your hand, holding the knife.

Reach up and grab hold of his wrist and turn under his arm to your right.

Now bend your arm toward his body, and he will not be able to stop you as you thrust the knife into his abdomen, then finish him with a stab to the back.

Defenses Against The Knife

A man attempts to stab at your abdomen. Lean back with your abdomen to give you more blocking room and do an X block in front of you on the man's wrist.

Continue to roll your wrists over to get him in a wrist lock (kotagasi). Now come back across your body, locking his wrist and throwing him to the ground.

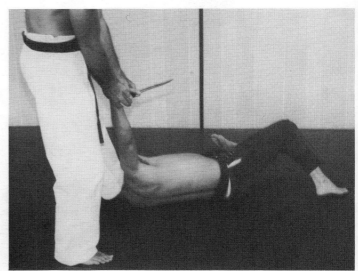

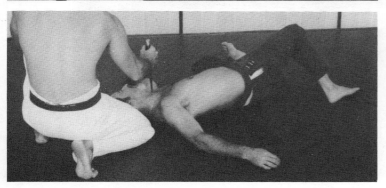

After he is on the ground break his wrist and take the knife. Finish him by stabbing his throat.

A man is attempting to slash you with the knife.

Move very fast as he moves at you and block the knife arm with your left forearm. Now quickly come up with a snap kick into his groin.

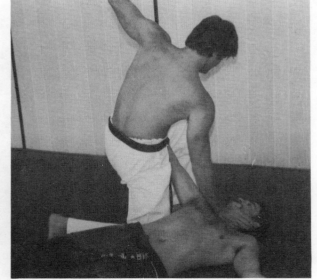

Knock him to the ground, and finish him with a shuto to the throat.

A man attempts to slash you with the knife.

Duck backwards very fast and let the slash go by, then move in to block the knife arm with your left forearm and right wrist before he can return to slash again.

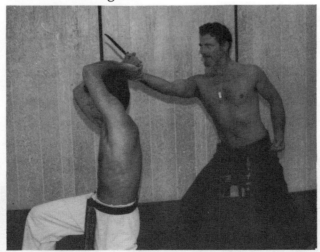

Lock his wrist up and drop to the ground taking your hands over your head and throwing him to the ground.

Closeup of wrist lock.

Throw him to the ground and take the knife and finish him by stabbing his throat.

A man attempts to stab you.

Block up with your left arm and reach behind with your right and lock his knife arm.

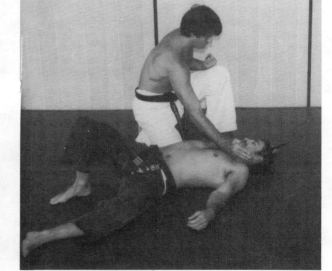

Throw him to the ground, and finish him with a shuto to the throat.

Using a Coat or Gi Top to Block the Knife Attack

Wrap the gi around your forearm and block up with it to stop the knife arm.

Counter with a snap kick to the groin, done very fast and hard.

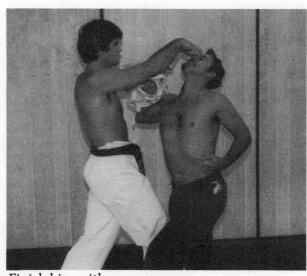

Finish him with an eye gouge.

A man attempts to stab at you.

Block his knife arm with a crescent kick to his forearm area. Do not kick the knife, this will cut you.

Finish him with a heel kick into his throat.

24

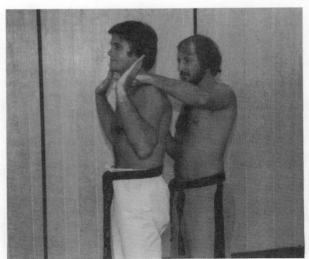

A man has a knife against your throat from behind. Always raise your arms as if giving up.

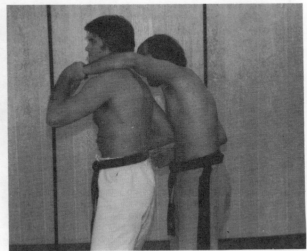

Grab his knife arm and elbow him with the left elbow.

Now step behind holding his knife arm.

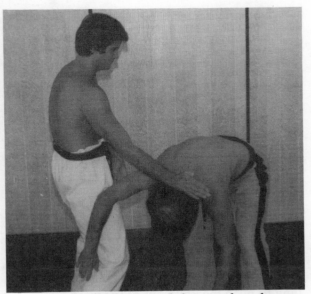

Continue to step and finish him with a shuto to the back of the neck.

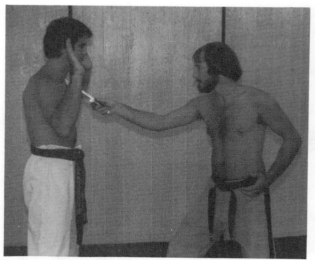

A man holds a knife at your throat from the front.

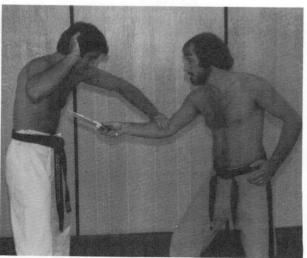

Quickly lean back with your abdomen and strike his forearm near the elbow with your left hand.

Before he can move kick his groin, while continuing to push the knife out of the way.

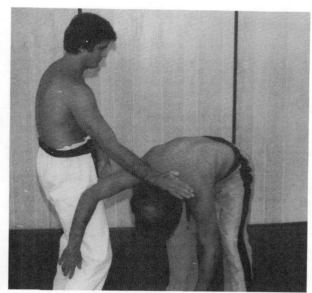

Finish him with a hard shuto to the neck.

A man holds a knife at your back. Raise your arms as if to give up.

Now quickly swing your left arm around back to knock the knife away and smash a heel kick into his groin.

Kata

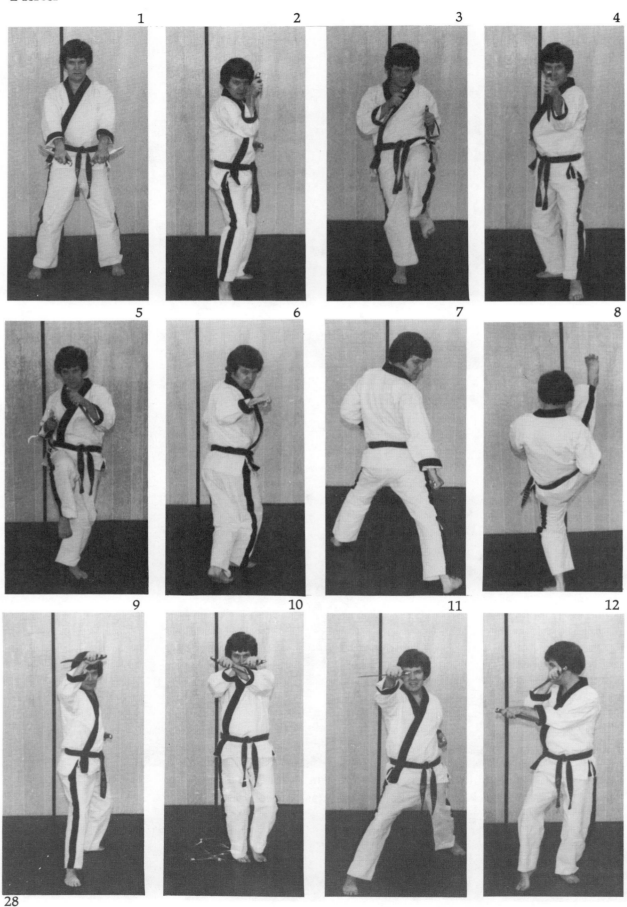

13

14

15

16

17

18

19

20

29

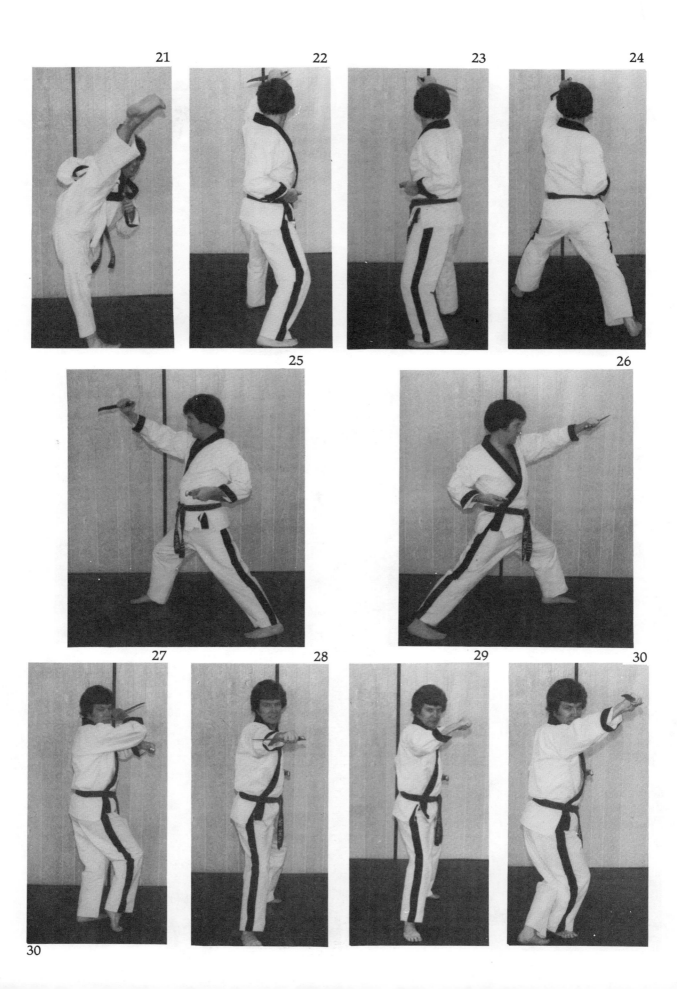

Chapter 2

The Yawara

The yawara is one of the forgotten weapons of karate but is one of the most effective and easy-to-use weapons available today. It consists of a hard piece of wood, usually white oak, that is from eight to six inches in length. The ends can be pointed but usually are blunted. The yawara is often found with eight sides for added control, but a rounded yawara is equally effective.

The yawara is used in combination with kicks and punches and strikes such areas as the eyes, ears, groin, throat, and other vital parts of the body. It can be used to attack nerves and pressure points and because of its small size is easily concealed for protection and convenience.

The yawara is carried by many police in the Orient and is used to control prisoners by applying it to nerve and pressure points, as well as to break up fights and for self-defense.

Holding Positions and Striking Areas

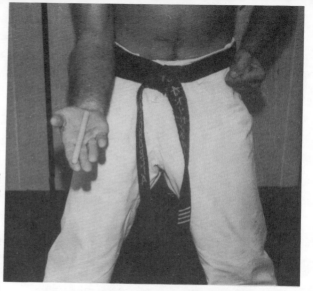

To grip the yawara, hold the stick in the middle of the palm of the hand so that the end of the stick is about at the end of your forefinger.

Now wrap the last three fingers of the hand around the stick, press the thumb against the side of the stick, and extend the forefinger down to the end of the yawara for control and concealment.

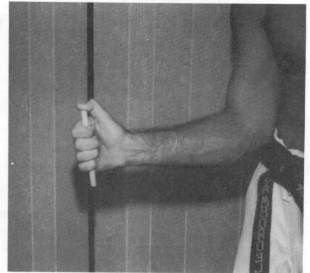

Another common holding position is to grip all fingers tightly around the stick and hold the thumb over the end for control, with about two inches extending out the other side of the palm.

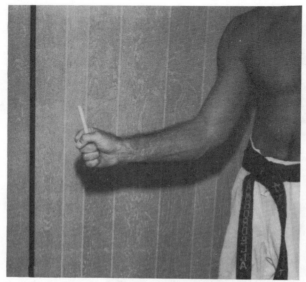

For striking areas such as the ears and throat, the entire hand may be wrapped around the stick with about one-half of the stick extending out the top of the hand.

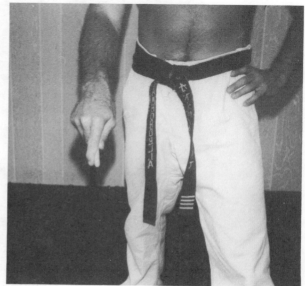

You can also use the stick to poke eyes by holding it with most of the stick extending down the forefinger and the thumb far down the side.

Striking Areas

Jam the end of the stick into the eyes.

Smash the stick into the bridge of the nose.

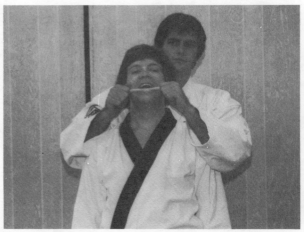

Pull the stick through the mouth, tearing the lips open.

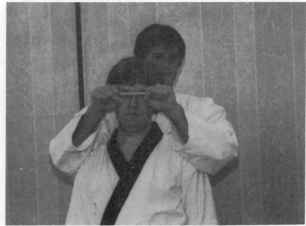

Pull the stick against the bridge of the nose, crushing it.

Force the stick into the ear.

Press the stick into the joint below the ear at the top of the jaw.

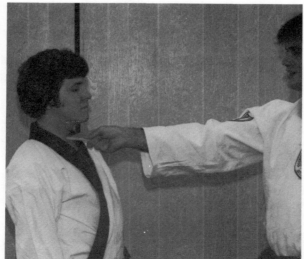

Jam the end of the stick into the bottom of the throat.

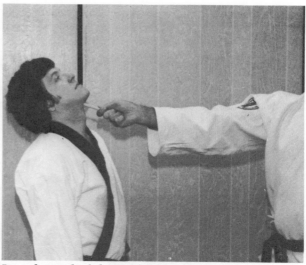

Jam the end of the stick into the lower jaw or top of the throat; this is a sensitive lymph gland.

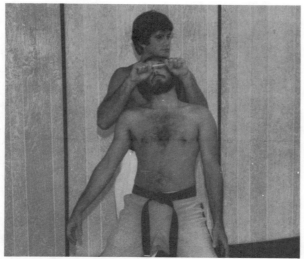

Using the yawara to hold a man by pressing against the bridge of the nose.

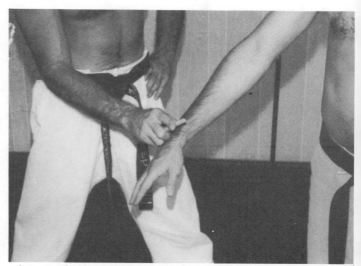

A wrist lock and pressure point. Begin by wrapping the stick across the top of the forearm, and press down very hard.

Now roll the forearm over and pull up and press into the wrist area with the yawara. This will cause pain and control the man or expose his ribs to a punch.

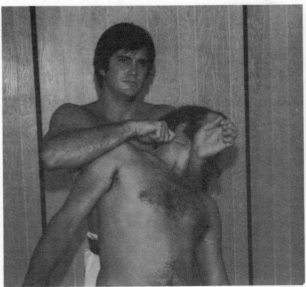

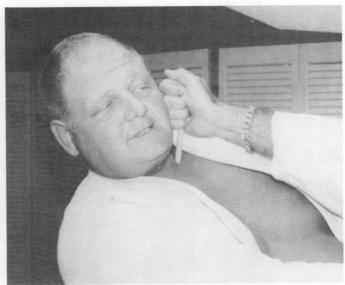

Holding a man by applying pressure against the gland at the top of the jaw and just below the ear. Press the end of the yawara into this sensitive area while holding the head and exposing the neck.

Press the end of the stick into the area above the collarbone. This will cause considerable pain.

Holding a large man against the wall by applying pressure against the top of the lips just under the nose with the yawara.

Simply take the yawara and smash the end of it into the back of the hand. This will break several bones of the hand and make him release you very fast.

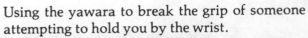

Using the yawara to break the grip of someone attempting to hold you by the wrist.

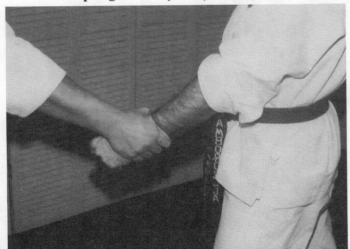

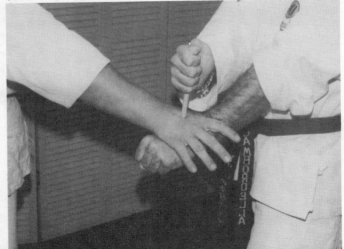

An example of blocking and then thrusting the end of the yawara into the throat to choke the man.

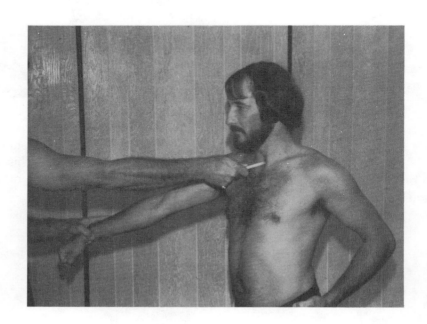

Applications and Techniques for Using the Yawara to Stop an Attack

A man attempts to grab you from the side; you stand natural with the yawara concealed in your right hand.

As he gets close to you, quickly turn to the right and smash the end of the stick into his eye, then push down. This will cause him to fall to the ground.

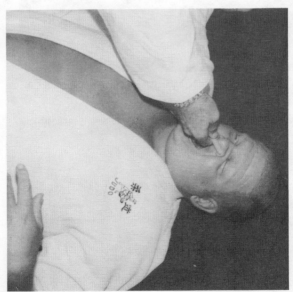

On the ground, you can tear off his nose or finish poking out his eye.

Blocking a punch: ready for the attack by holding the yawara in the right hand.

Block the punch with your left hand using a middle block.

Counter by thrusting the end of the yawara into his eye.

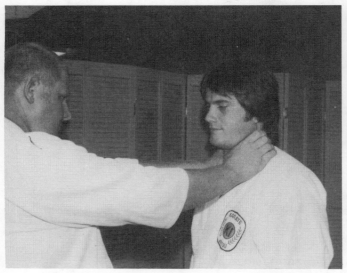

Using the yawara to break a front choke.

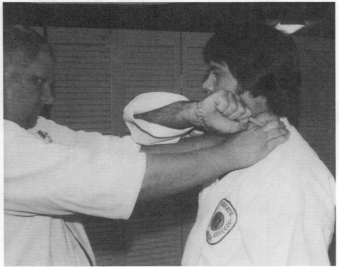

Smash the end of the yawara into the back of his hands near the fingers.

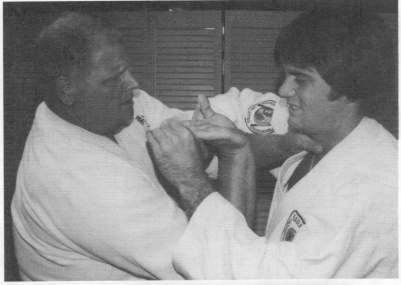

Now pull off his hand and put the yawara through his fingers, twisting it while holding the fingers together. This is very painful.

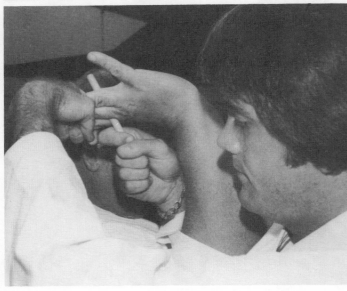

Close-up of the yawara between the fingers; note the fingers being held together and the yawara being twisted.

As a man attempts to punch at you, administer a pressing low block with your left hand.

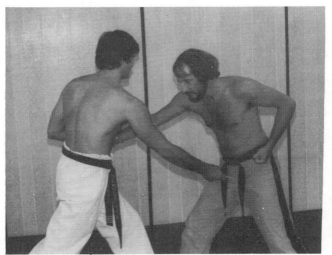

Counter by thrusting the yawara into his groin.

Finish by coming up and smashing the yawara into his throat.

42

Block the punch with your left hand and ready the yawara in your right.

Smash the yawara into his solar plexus.

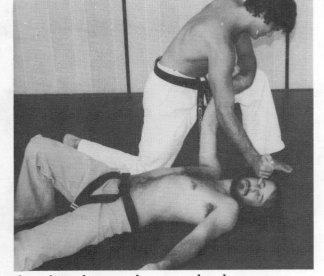

Come down with the yawara onto his collar bone, knocking him to the ground, where you finish him with a thrust into his eye.

A man attempts to snap a kick at you.

Block the kick with your left hand and smash the yawara onto his shin.

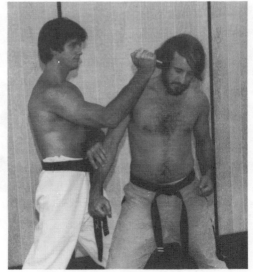

Finish him by smashing the yawara into his ear.

Using the Yawara
to Break Up a Fight

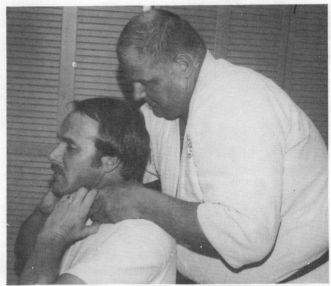

A large man is choking a smaller man and will
not let go.

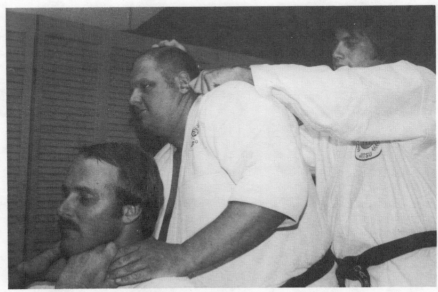

Come up from behind and grab his hair. Smash the end of the
yawara into his ear, pressing into his ear and pulling back. He
will let go, but you should be prepared to stop him.

Kata

13

14

15

16

17

18

19

20

21

22

23

Chapter 3

The Tonfa

The tonfa is often referred to as the "rice grinder" because that was the original purpose for which the stick was devised. The tonfa is still used today to grind rice in many parts of the world. It is composed of a hard piece of wood, usually white oak, and measures about seventeen inches in length. The handle is approximately four and one-half inches, and the entire weapon weighs about one and one-half pounds. It can be used singly or doubly as a weapon both for self-defense and for attack.

The size and structure of the tonfa allow the user to combine speed and power together with his own agility and ability to become a dangerous fighting machine. Although it is extremely effective, it is difficult to master completely and so is often not taught to beginners. Its popularity has increased in the last few years, and because it is inexpensive and easy to maintain, I am certain that its popularity will continue to grow.

When practicing with the tonfa, one should take care to use as much control and focus as possible to generate the full power potential of the weapon. It takes practice to learn to swing and snap the weapon with force, but once mastered, the tonfa is a formidable weapon of defense.

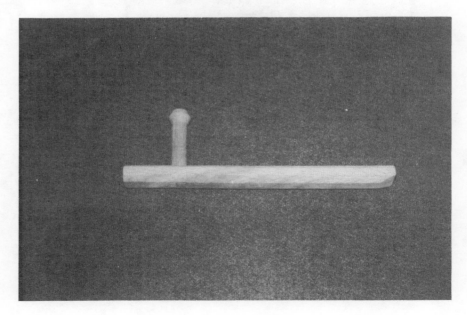

Holding the Tonfa

The tonfa should be gripped by the handle with a standard holding grip, and the length of the stick should extend down the forearm.

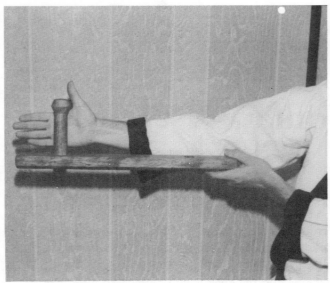

Steps: Take the tonfa and hold it down your forearm. Place the handle in the middle of your palm.

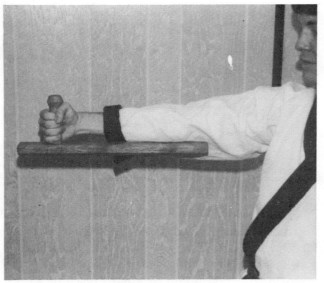

Close the grip around the tonfa, locking the thumb over the fingers and keeping the wrist straight so that the stick stays down the forearm.

Front view of the gripping.

Flipping the Tonfa

The power of most strikes with the tonfa comes from flipping the sticks out and then smashing them into vital areas of the body. Thus, one should practice the flip until he masters it with both hands.

Steps: Hold the tonfa in the right or left hand with the length extending down the forearm.

Now flip the wrist very hard to the right while you slightly loosen the grip to let the weapon turn in your palm.

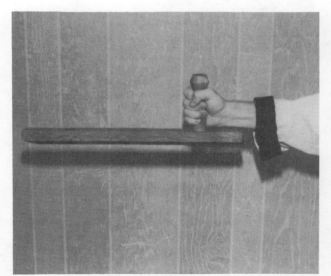

When the stick is all the way out in front, tighten the grip and strike or block. Then loosen

the grip and flip the wrist again to the right, allowing the stick to return to the starting or holding position.

Blocks

The tonfa is quite effective when blocking and is simply used as an extension of the forearm when the standard karate blocks are performed.

The high block or rising block: raise the arm up quickly and forcefully in front of the face; be sure to keep the tonfa snug to the forearm.

The middle block: bring the tonfa across the body and snap it in front of the chest.

The low block or groin block: snap the tonfa down across the groin.

X block for groin: used to block a strong kick. Cross the tonfas in front of the groin.

X block or rising X: used to block a strong shuto or weapon attack. Snap the tonfas up and cross them in front of the face.

Side block: used to block a kick or punch. Snap the arm to the side, keeping the tonfa snug to the forearm.

Cat stance block: turn the left arm horizontally and snug the right arm to the body.

Back block and strike: the tonfa is held and thrust to the back for a block and strike.

Striking Areas
and Striking Positions

Double strike to sides of face: both sticks are snapped into the sides of the face.

Knee strike: snap the tonfa down and smash the kneecap.

Backward thrust: into abdomen or groin area.

Groin smash: snap the stick up into the groin.

Nose smash: use the heel of the tonfa and smash into the bridge of the nose.

Teeth smash: smash the handle of the tonfa into the teeth.

Throat strike: swing the tonfa across the side of the neck.

Face smash: use the heel of the tonfa to smash into the face and mouth area.

Techniques of Defense with the Tonfa

Prepare for the attack by holding the tonfa in both hands in a modified cat stance.

Block the punch with a rising block with the left tonfa, then counter with a throat thrust with the right tonfa.

Follow with a smash into the temples with the left tonfa, and finish with a smash of the right tonfa to the side of the face.

Ready for the attack; stand in a modified cat stance.

Block the strike with the left tonfa in a rising block. Counter with a smash of the heel of the

tonfa in the right hand into the attacker's stomach.

Follow with a heel smash of the left tonfa into the side of the jaw, and finish with a flip and smash with the right tonfa into the teeth.

Ready for the attack with a cat stance.

Block the punch with a middle block across the body with the left tonfa. Counter with a flip smash into the ribs with the right tonfa.

Finish with a smash with the left tonfa into the teeth and face, knocking the attacker to the ground. Smash the right tonfa across the side of the head.

Ready for the attack.

Block the snap kick to the groin with the left tonfa in a groin block. Counter with a smash

with the heel of the right tonfa into the ribs and stomach.

Follow with a smash of the heel of the left tonfa into the throat, knocking your attacker to the

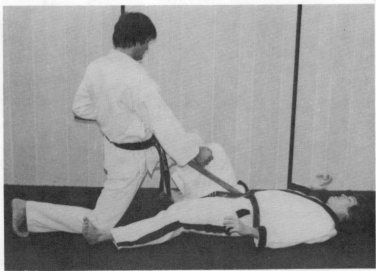

ground. Finish with a smash into the groin with the right tonfa.

Ready to block a kick attack.

Block the snap kick with an X block in front of the groin.

Counter with a double smash with both tonfas into the eyes.

Finish with a smash of the right tonfa into the side of the head.

Ready to block the roundhouse kick.

Block with a double middle block using both tonfas, and counter with a flip smash with the right tonfa into the side of the head.

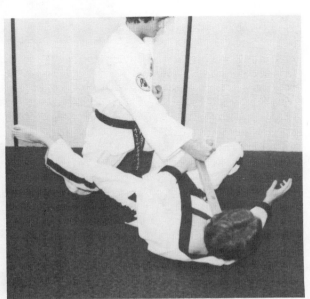

Grab the top of his gi with your right hand and lock your left leg behind his right. Throw him to the ground, where you finish him with a smash with the right tonfa into the face.

Ready to block a side kick.

Smash the right tonfa down into the side of the leg, blocking the kick and causing your attacker to drop his kicking leg. Counter with a flip smash with the left tonfa into the back of the head.

Ready to block the kick.

Block the roundhouse with the right tonfa against the shin, and use the left tonfa to block the punch.

Counter by spinning and thrusting the left tonfa into the stomach.

Finish with a heel kick to the throat.

Block an attack with the bo using the tonfas.

Block the overhead strike with an X rising block.

Counter by pushing the bo down with the left tonfa, and smash the right tonfa into the side of the head.

Finish by thrusting the heel of the left tonfa into the face and striking the back of the head with the right tonfa.

Defenses Against the Tonfa

Preparing to block the tonfa by assuming a modified cat stance.

Block the strike with the left tonfa with a pressing block with the right hand.

Counter and finish with a left elbow smash into the throat.

Preparing to block the tonfas.

Block the right tonfa with a rising block with the left arm, and block the left tonfa with a rising block with the right arm.

Counter with a snap kick to the groin, and finish with a double shuto to the collarbones.

Preparing to block the tonfas.

Use a left crescent kick to strike the left tonfa and arm as he attempts to strike you.

Counter with a side kick into the throat.

Using a Bo to Defend Against the Tonfas

Prepare to block the tonfa with the bo by holding the bo in the right arm.

Block the right tonfa with a downward strike with the bo.

Counter by smashing the bo into the right side.

Finish by smashing the bo into the side of the head.

Prepare to block the tonfa with the bo by holding the bo in the right arm.

Block the strike with the left tonfa with a side block with the bo.

Counter with a smash into the ribs.

Finish with a smash to the side of the head.

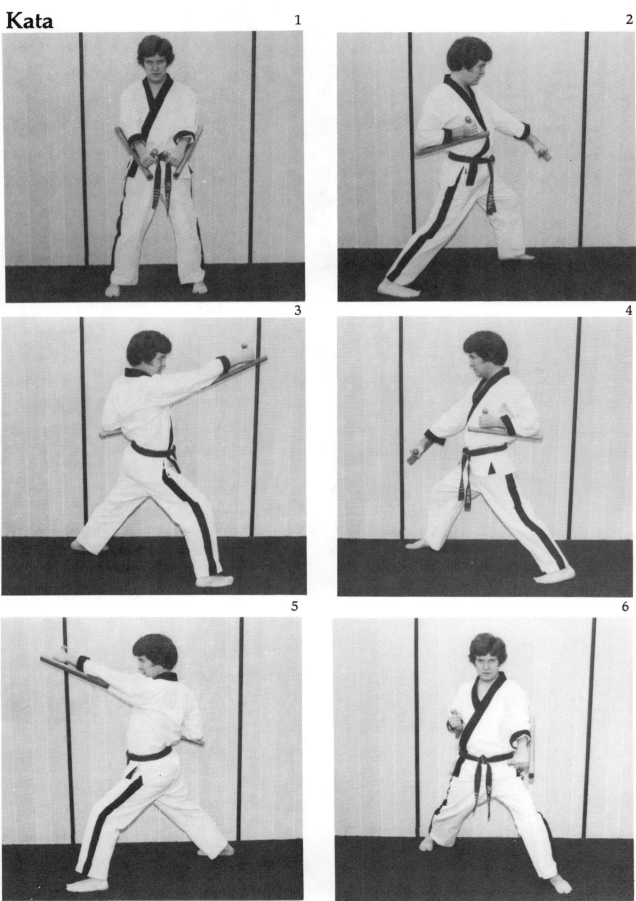

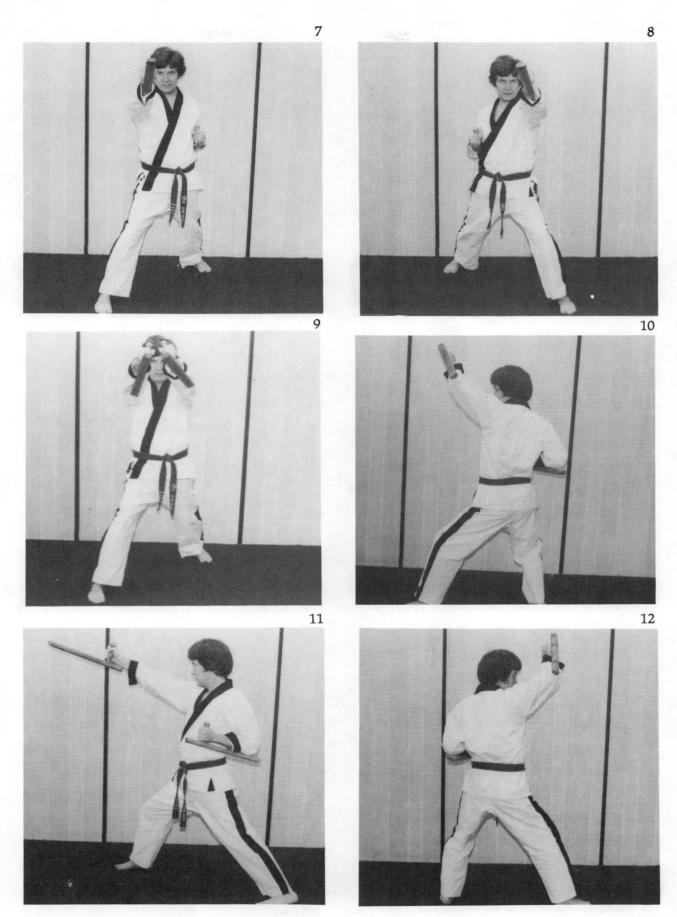

explanation of preceding move   15   16

17   18

Chapter 4

The Staff

The staff is called by many names, the baton, the jo, the night stick, the bat, but all refer to a stick of wood that is approximately two to three feet in length. It is a very common weapon of defense and is carried by most of the police in the world because of its effectiveness.

It can be used to strike, to block, to jab, to hold, and to throw an opponent and is easily made and maintained. With a little practice you will be able to twirl the stick in your hands and around your body and make yourself into a formidable weapon of defense.

Because the staff is hard, and because most of the strikes go to soft and vulnerable areas of the body, I recommend that you practice most of your techniques with a rubber stick or hollow tube until you have mastered your basics and acquired enough control for safety.

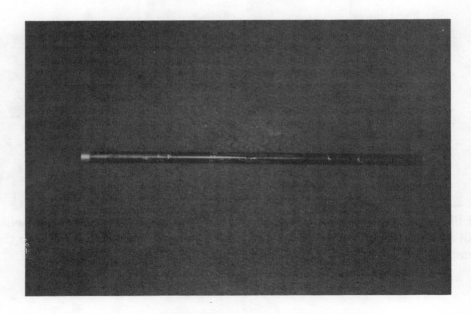

Holding the Staff

The staff should not be held in the middle but rather held so that much more of the stick extends out one end of the hand than the other. Usually this can be done by holding approximately twelve inches, then the grip, and the other twenty-four inches extending out.

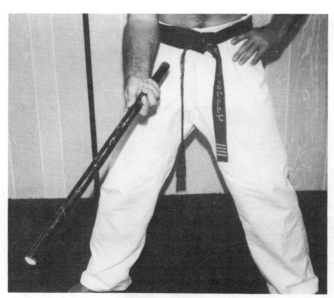

Grip the staff like you would a tennis racquet, holding it with all four fingers wrapped around it and the thumb riding on the top, or wrapped around the fingers. Here we see the staff being held out in front of the body (where the thumb is wrapped on top) and held to the side (where the thumb is around the fingers).

Holding the staff behind for striking and blocking, using a closed grip. The staff extended out for a strike or a block.

Blocking Positions

The two-handed groin block or X block: snap the staff down in front of the groin with both hands holding the staff.

The groin block (open). Here the staff snaps to block the groin, but the arms are not crossed.

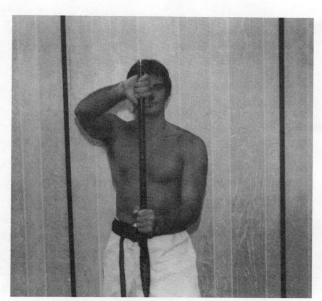

The two-handed side block: snap the staff across the body and block the chest area (front view of front block).

The side block.

The high block or rising block with two hands: snap the staff up to block the head with both hands holding the staff.

The groin-striking block: swing the staff down in front of the groin with both hands to effect a swinging block.

The one-handed rising block: snap the arm up to block the face with the staff held down the forearm.

The front-rising block: snap up the staff with one arm to block the front of the body holding the staff down the forearm.

The swinging or striking low block: swing the staff down across the leg to block a kick.

The striking rising block: snap the staff across and in front of the body to block kicks and punches.

The middle-striking block: snap the staff in front of the chest to block the abdomen.

The striking groin block: snap the staff across the front of the lower body to block the groin.

Blocking Demonstrated

The rising block with two hands: the staff is snapped up to block the strike.

The middle block with one hand: the staff strikes the punching arm.

The double groin block: the staff snaps down to block the kick to the groin.

The side two-handed block: the staff snaps to the side to block the kick.

The side block with one hand: the staff swings down and strikes the kicking leg.

The middle block with one arm: the staff swings across the body to contact and block the punch.

Striking Areas

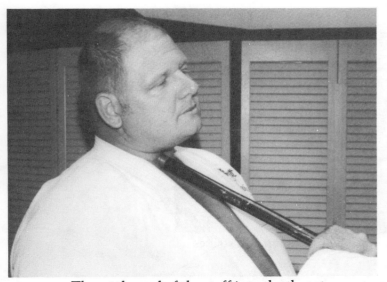

Thrust the end of the staff into the eye.

Thrust the end of the staff into the throat.

Smash the side of the face with the staff.

86

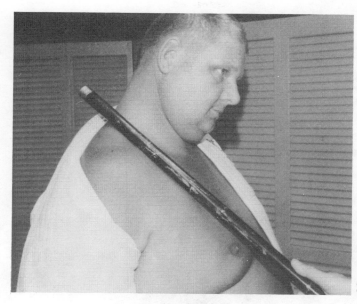

Smash the collarbone with the staff.

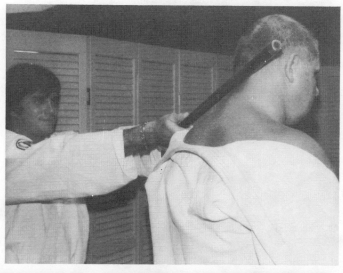

Smash the back of the neck or spine with the staff.

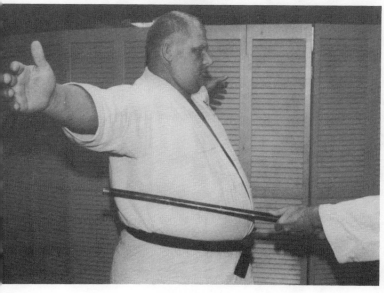

Smash the ribs (floating) with the staff.

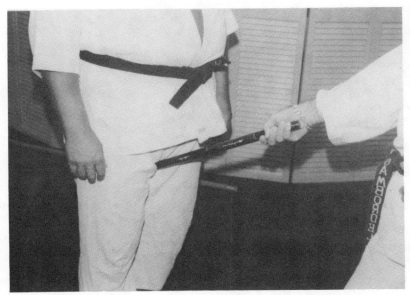

Smash up into the groin.

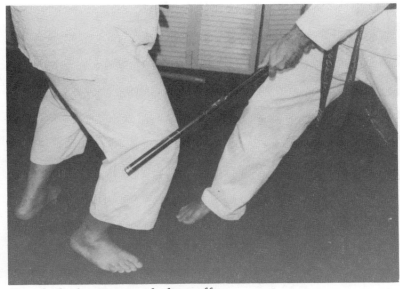

Smash the kneecap with the staff.

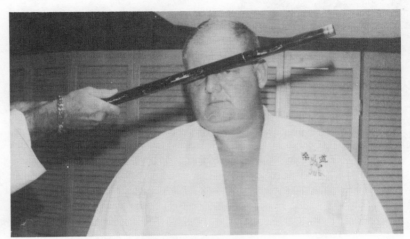

Smash between the eyes with the staff.

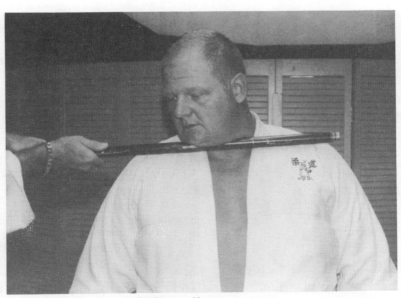

Smash the throat with the staff.

To develop proper power when striking with the staff always swing the hips, just like on a punch. Ready for smash to the front.

Smash the staff across the body and to the front. Notice the hip swing.

Flipping the staff sideways for a front strike.

Notice the wrist flips the staff around to the front.

Thrusting the staff forward.

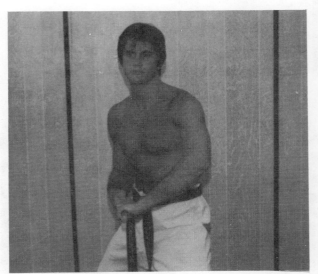

Front view.

Jabbing with the staff.

Side view.

Striking with the Staff: How to Get More Power and Greater Range

Often when striking with the staff a simple block can stop your attack, so the following techniques can overcome these blocks and still effect a strike that will disable.

You attempt to do an overhead strike to the head of an opponent, but he blocks with a rising block.

To overcome this, simply flip up on your wrist and this will cause his block to fall short.

Closeups of why the new strike works to give greater distance. The first strike is blocked.

The wrist is flipped up, and the second strike hits the target.

You attempt to strike the side of an opponent's head, but he counters with a forearm block.

Simply flip out and extend the wrist, and you can still strike the head despite the block.

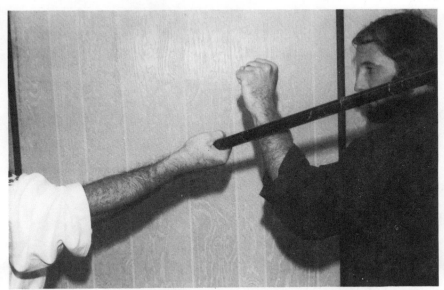

Closeup of the wrist flip-out, to give greater striking range. The first strike is blocked.

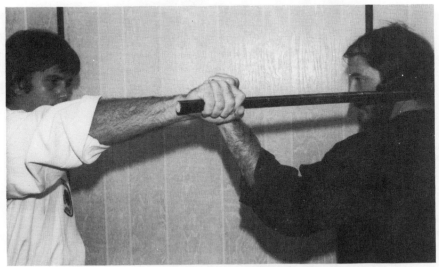

The second strike hits the head, because the wrist is flipped out to the side to give greater striking distance.

Techniques of Using the Staff for Defending Oneself Against an Unarmed Opponent

Technique 1: ready position, staff is concealed down the right leg.

As he strikes you, smash the staff down onto his striking arm, then grasp arm with left hand.

Now smash staff into his knees, causing him to drop to the ground, where you finish with a smash to the head.

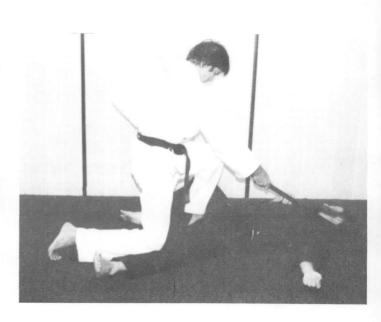

Technique 2: ready for strike, with staff concealed down right leg.

As he strikes, smash his left elbow with staff.

Come back and around with staff and smash staff into his kidneys.

Finish by smashing his neck with staff.

Technique 3: ready for strike, standing left with staff hidden down right leg.

As he strikes, block across with left hand and grasp wrist.

Now take both hands and jab end of staff into his eyes.

Technique 4: ready position for grabbing attack, staff hidden down right side.

As he reaches, thrust out staff into solar plexus, then up with right smash across the side of his face.

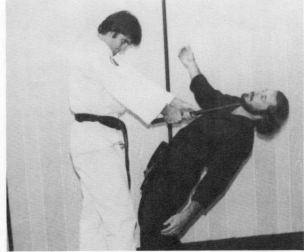

Now finish by kicking snap-kick to groin, then smashing staff down into throat and side of neck.

Technique 5: as he prepares to strike you this time, you hold staff in left hand under arm.

When he starts his strike, thrust staff out into his throat, then flip up into his face.

Now smash staff down into his knee, which is exposed, causing him to lean, and you strike his neck as he falls over.

Technique 6: as opponent reaches from behind you to grab you, you are ready with staff down right side.

Flip staff up straight over your head, striking his head with staff.

Finish by drawing back the staff and smashing the groin area of the attacker.

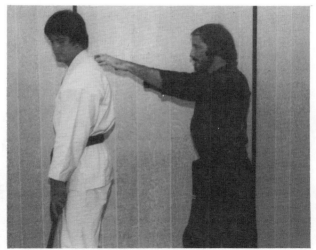

Technique 7: opponent is reaching from behind you to grab you; you have staff in left hand.

Step to the left side and thrust backwards with the staff into his abdomen.

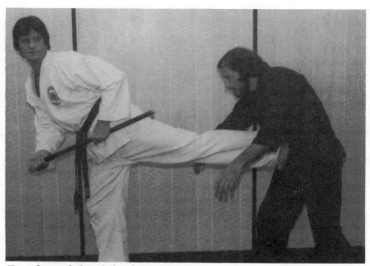

Finish with back kick into groin.

Technique 8: using the staff for a throw and break; opponent is preparing to strike you, hold staff down right leg.

As he strikes, smash into elbow area of his attacking arm, then reach up and lock arm with staff.

Now throw backwards and snap arm by pulling up very hard on staff as you throw.

Using the Staff to Block and Counter an Attack with the Bo

Opponent prepares to strike at you with the bo. Hold staff in front of body with both hands.

As he strikes with bo, bring staff up with double-hand block and stop bo.

Now continue to come across and strike the back of his head with the staff, then come down and smash his knee.

Technique 2 against bo: opponent prepares to strike with bo. Staff is held behind with one hand.

As he strikes, swing staff across and contact bo away from body on your left side.

Finish with a side kick to the side of his head.

Defenses Against the Staff

Opponent prepares to strike you with an overhead strike.

Block up before his strike gets too far down with a rising block near his wrist. Now lock your hands on his arms and throw him to the ground.

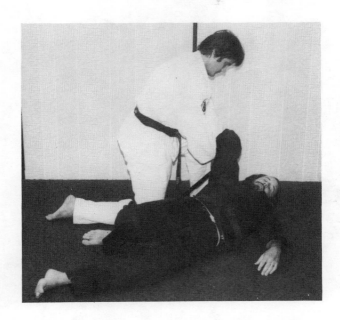

After throwing him to the ground, break his
arm by snapping up on it, take the staff and
smash into his throat to finish him.

Opponent prepares to jab your stomach with the staff. As he thrusts, do an X block out in front of your body.

Now continue your movement to the right and bring his arms up, locking his wrist with your hands.

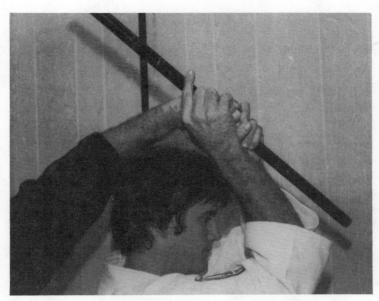

Closeup of wrist-locking technique. Throw him
to the ground.

Take the staff and smash in the back of his head.

Attacker prepares to smash the staff into the side of your body.

Move quickly and stop his arm before he can get too close to your side by striking his arm near the elbow and upper arm. Use both hands to stop his movement.

Now grab around his head with your right arm and pull his body to you and throw him to the

ground using a hip throw. There you can finish him with a stomp to the throat.

Attacker attempts to smash a backhand into your face.

Block using both hands, the left near the elbow and the right near the wrist.

Now continue to hold his right wrist with your hands and drop to one knee moving over and down with your hold and throwing him to the ground. There take the staff and smash his face.

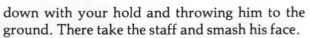

Blocking the Staff
with Kicking Techniques

Attacker attempts to jab at your stomach.

Sidestep and thrust a left side kick into his groin and rib area.

Attacker attempts to smash at your side with staff.

Block the staff with a crescent kick using your right foot.

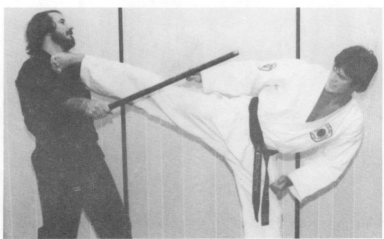

Then with the same foot snap your leg back up and into his face and throat to finish him.

113

Attacker attempts to strike with the staff at your head.

Come up with a high front snap and catch his arm around the elbow area and stop the staff.

Now snap a front groin-kick up with the right leg and finish him.

You are being choked from behind with the staff: two escapes and counters.

Lift both arms up and grasp the staff to relieve the choking pressure, then smash the elbow of

the right arm down and into his stomach. Finish him with a kick.

Or, hold the staff and pull down to relieve the choking pressure. Then throw him over your head to the ground and stomp him to finish him.

Using a Jumping Spin-Kick to Stop an Attack with the Staff

(Note: this is a beautiful kick but takes a very long time to master.)

As the attacker attempts to strike your leg with the staff, jump straight up.

Then turn your back and spin all the way around 360 degrees.

Come down across his face with the heel of your foot and disable him.

Kata

1

2

3

4

5

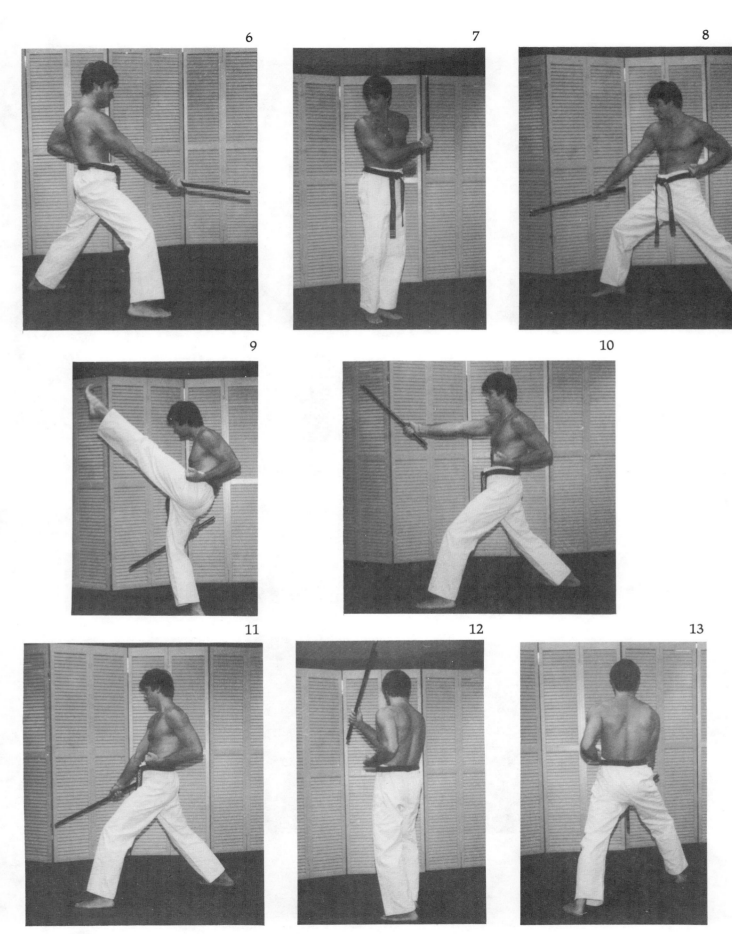

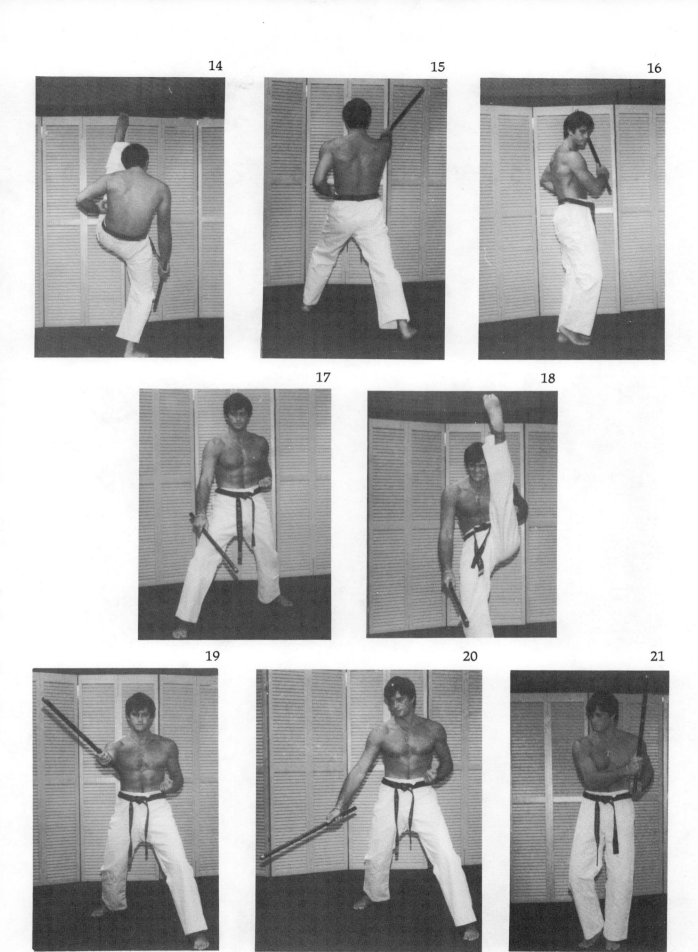

14

15

16

17

18

19

20

21

22

23

24

25

26

27

28

29

30

31

Chapter 5
The Bo

The bo is an excellent weapon but one of the more impractical ones because of its size. It is a piece of hard wood about six feet in length, and therefore cannot be easily concealed or carried in a car or on your person. Still, it has remained a favorite karate weapon for years because of its versatility and beauty when used in the hands of a master.

Because of its length, the bo is often used to block nunchaku, or knives or other weapons, and techniques of the bo are used today by most military forces when they teach rifle or punja stick fighting. The original bo was used for a walking stick and for a prod for cattle or goats but became a weapon in the hands of the skilled martial artist.

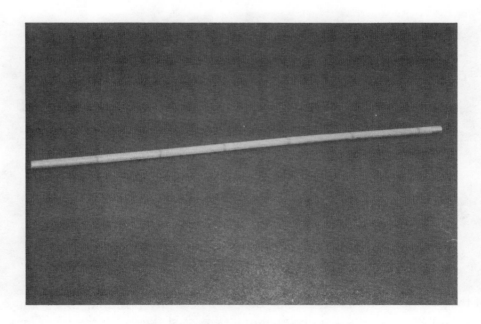

Holding the Bo

There are several different methods of holding the bo, but the most common one used for defense is the stance with the bo held in the hand by the side.

Steps: stand with the feet shoulder-width apart, with the bo held in the right hand and going down the side of the right leg. The hand should be placed around the bo, with the palm facing away from the body.

Side view of the holding stance. Note that the hand is wrapped around the bo with the fingers pointing down and the thumb wrapped around the front.

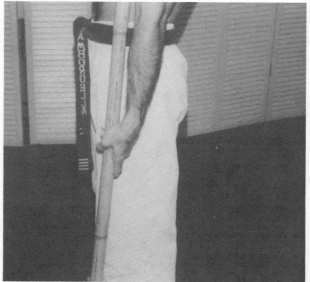

Close-up of the position of the hand holding the bo. The fingers are wrapped around the bo, and the forefinger is extended slightly downward. The thumb is securely wrapped around, and the bo rests against the leg.

The ready position: this is the stance used for most strikes with the bo. The left hand comes across the chest and wraps around the bo with the palm facing away from the body. The right hand is in the position we have already seen.

Blocks

The two-handed groin block: used for strong kicks. Step forward with either leg, and thrust the bo down squarely in front of the groin.

The middle block with two hands: swing the bo across the chest and snap it in front of the body to block punches and kicks.

The low block: snap the bo downward and to the side in front of the legs and groin area.

Rising block with two hands: snap up the bo directly in front of the head.

The two-hand extended groin block: used to strike and block kicks from a greater distance.

Thrusting the bo across the body for a strike: stand in a side stance with the bo equally in front of you.

Now step to the side and thrust both arms across the body, snapping the bo out to the side.

Close-up of the hand position in the side thrust.

The overhead strike: stand with the bo in the ready position. The right hand holds the bo low, and the left hand is across the body.

Flip the right hand up toward the front in a circle while pulling across and down with the left hand.

Front view.

Snap the bo straight out and lock it under the arm of the left hand.

Side View.

127

Picking the bo up off the floor without using your hands: if you should find yourself in the position of having a bo on the ground and still having to defend yourself, and you cannot bend over to get it, you can pick it up with your feet. Roll the bottom of the foot on top of the bo while keeping up your guard.

Now quickly, but smoothly, roll the foot back, and the bo will roll up on top of your foot.

Now lift the knee straight up, and the bo will fly up into the air. You can catch it with your left hand. It takes practice, and you must be sure to pick the bo up as near the center as possible lest it fly up crooked.

Techniques for Using the Bo

Prepare for the attack: the bo is held in the right hand down the leg.

As he punches, swing the bo out and into his ribs.

Now flip the bo around and smash his other side. This will knock him down.

Finish him with a smash to the face and throat.

Ready for the attack.

As he punches, thrust the bo out and into his abdomen.

Now quickly come up and smash the side of his face.

Follow with a smash to the other side and finish him off.

Ready to block a kick.

Now flip the bow upward and into the groin.

Block the snap kick by swinging the bo downward across the foot.

Then thrust the bo up into the throat.

Finish with a smash to the neck and shoulder.

131

Block the snap kick with a two-handed groin block.

Take the left hand off and flip the bo with the right hand under the leg.

Continue to go around. This will lock the leg so that you can throw him to the ground.

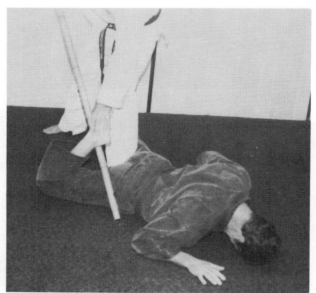

On the ground, break his leg by holding his foot and applying pressure with the bo.

Using the Bo for Defense Against Other Weapons

Against an attack with the tonfas: ready for the attack.

Block the strike with the left tonfa by striking the bo against his arm.

Block the counter with the right tonfa by swinging the bo across to catch it and stop it.

Finish him by smashing the bo down on his head.

Against the Sai

Ready to block the sai.

Block the right sai by swinging the bo across the body.

Block the left sai by swinging the bo back to the left.

Counter by striking the side of his head.

Finish by smashing his face with a left-hand swing.

Against the Knife

Ready to block the knife.

Block his thrust by swinging the bo downward across his knife arm.

Counter and finish him by smashing upward with the bo into the side of his face.

Ready to block the knife.

Block his stab with a two-handed rising block.

Counter with a smash to the side of his head.

Finish him with a smash on the back of his neck.

Ready to block the baton.

Swing the bo across the body and contact the baton to stop it.

Counter with a smash to the side of the head.

Finish with a two-handed overhead smash to the back.

Using the Bo to Throw an Opponent

As the man prepares to attack you, stand to the side with the bo across your body. As he starts to move, thrust the bo across your body and between his arm and back.

Now throw him by swinging the bo up over his head and then in a large circle to the ground. This can also be used to break or dislocate his shoulder if done with speed and snapping action.

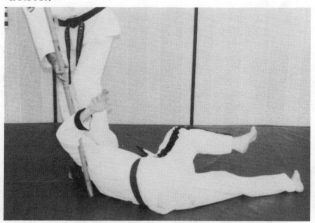

Defense Against the Bo

Escape from a rear choke with the bo: as he chokes you from behind, tighten your neck muscles.

Now bring up your arms and pull down on the bo to relieve the choking pressure.

Hold very tight and bend your knees and lift. This will throw him over your back to the ground.

On the ground, you will find you have the bo. Use it to smash his groin.

Blocking the Bo with a Kicking Attack

As the attacker swings at you, get ready to kick the bo.

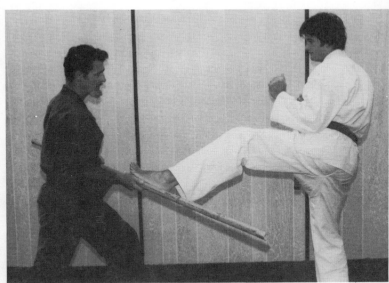

Quickly swing up the left leg and contact the bo and his right hand with the ball of your foot.

Quickly drop your leg and face backward to the man.

Before he can move, snap a back kick into his jaw.

An attacker swings the bo at your side.

Swing your body around in a circle to the left and grab the bo with both hands. You must move very fast, but you can do it.

Now grab his shoulder and lift with your right leg and throw him to the ground.

On the ground, crush his chest with your knee and strike his throat with a shuto.

Using a Flying Kick to Block a Bo Attack

To do these techniques, you must be able to do flying kicks with speed, power, and accuracy.

The man attempts to strike you with the bo.

Jump up very high and let the bo pass underneath you.

Now thrust a flying side kick into his face.

146

The man attempts to strike you with the bo.

Jump straight up with both feet so that the bo goes underneath you.

Now thrust out both feet into his face.

Kata

7

8

9

10

149

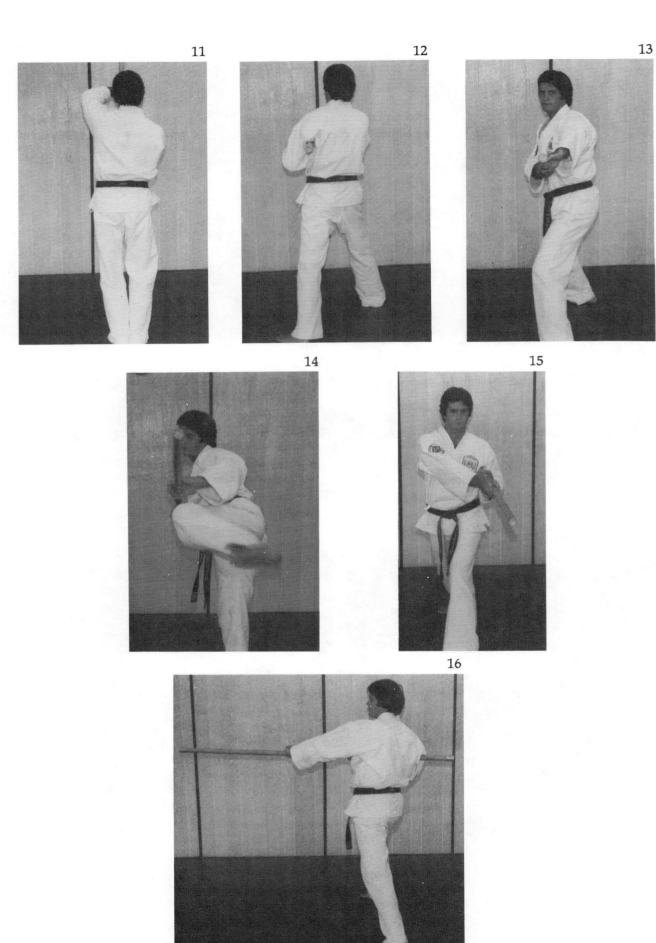

17

18

19

20

21

151

Chapter 6
The Nunchaku

Perhaps the most popular, purely martial arts weapon today are the nunchaku, and the reasons are numerous. Extremely effective and powerful, the nunchaku do not require great strength or skill to master. They are lightning fast and beautiful to watch, and so powerful that they allow the user to devastate several unarmed men at once. Therefore, they are illegal in many states, and will be in many more as they fall into the hands of unscrupulous users who employ them to hurt and kill other men instead of using them to practice the martial arts.

The sticks are really very simple but can be made quite complex. They consist of two pieces of hardwood, usually between ten and twelve inches long, held together by a piece of string, leather, or a chain.

Because the nunchaku are illegal to carry in many states, I suggest that you check with your local law enforcement agency before carrying them even to and from class.

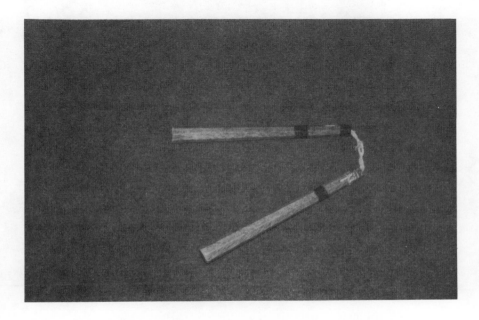

Holding the Nunchaku

Although many people prefer to hold the nunchaku down near the end of the sticks, I have found the area that gives you the most control and speed is to hold the nunchaku where they are balanced in your hand.

To find the balance point lie the sticks across the finger until they are balancing on the finger. I have marked my sticks with a piece of tape at this point for future reference.

Now close your hand around the sticks like you were holding a tennis racquet, extending the thumb and forefinger up the grip a little for control.

This is the grip from which most of your moves will be made, but there are other ways to hold the sticks and other strikes, so let's look at a few.

The front spread: for an eye strike. Hold the sticks in one hand with the sticks side by side in your hand.

Now roll your hand across the stick, pushing your thumb and fingers apart. This will open the front of the sticks for an eye strike.

You can also open the sticks using two hands, and this position can be used for blocks and strikes to the eyes, throat, neck, and leg.

The backward spread: hold the sticks in your hand with the string end facing your body and both sticks side by side.

Now roll your hand so the thumb and fingers spread apart, and this will open the sticks to the back. This can be used for striking or blocking.

Holding the Sticks on Your Body

Since the nunchaku are illegal to carry, I will not discuss carrying them concealed, but you should know how to carry them in class when you practice with them.

The front carry: place the sticks into your belt with the string end pointed down. This allows you easy access to the sticks.

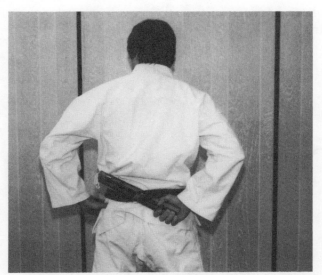

The back carry: place the sticks with the string area up top and under your belt across your back. This allows you to be able to reach around behind and grab the sticks.

Moving the Sticks

There are many different movement patterns you can practice with the sticks, and some of them are not functional, such as the swing and catch around the neck. Let's look at some of the better ones.

The figure 8: this is the most common movement and most versatile. It is used in most strikes and defenses. Stand with the feet shoulder-width apart and hold the sticks in either hand; keep the other hand up for blocking. Now begin to make a large figure 8 in front of the body.

As you get better, make the figure 8 smaller and faster, practice with both hands.

Take care to keep the swing wide enough not to hit the elbow, and far enough away from the body that you don't hit your face.

Behind the Back
Swing and Catch

Start out by making several figure 8s in front of the body, then take the sticks up over the head and drop and catch them behind the back.

Practice with both hands. Try to drop the sticks straight over the head. This makes the drop uniform and the catch easier.

Keep the catching hand wide open until you feel the sticks hit it. This prevents broken fingers.

Behind the Arm
Catch and Hold

This is most commonly used for defense, and almost all your defense positions come from this position, so practice it well.

Start out by holding the sticks in front of the body. Now take the right arm and bend it up, while pulling the left arm across the front of the chest and toward the back.

Now you have the sticks being held behind the arm, with the right arm up and wrist back to hold the sticks, and the left arm down low across the chest.

You must now practice this so you can do it while swinging the sticks. Do a loop up in front of the arm and catch the stick behind it.

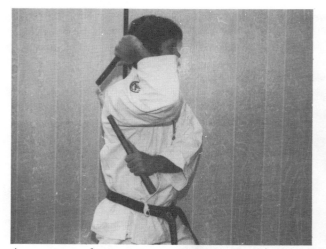 

As you get better you can make figure 8s in front, then flip the stick up and behind the arm to catch it.

Swinging the Sticks
Across the Body: for
Strikes and Blocks

You have to learn to do this so that you do not hit yourself with the sticks and so that you can get power.

Start by holding the sticks behind your back and over your shoulder, now bring them across your body (very slowly while you learn). Make

sure to snap the wrists directly in front of the body, and not near the end, or the sticks will hit you in the back.

Practice with both hands, and as you get better increase your speed and power.

The other arm should be kept in front for balance and blocking, and the shoulders slightly turn to move the sticks faster and keep them under more control as they cross the body.

Swinging the Sticks
Straight Down

This is a great strike, but you must practice slowly and easily so you do not hit yourself in the shin or groin.

Start with the sticks behind your back.

Now slowly swing the sticks down in front of you until they go between your legs. Snap the sticks in front of the body, not near the legs or you will hit your back, shin or groin. Make sure to point the wrist down and be sure to always aim the wrist between the legs so the sticks may pass there smoothly.

Practice with both hands. Only go faster when you can do it blindfolded and not hit yourself. In fact, all of the moves you practice you should be able to do blindfolded.

Catching the Sticks Between the Legs

Needless to say, you had better start out slowly and keep going very slow, if you want to have babies.

Start to learn by just dropping the sticks down between the legs and grabbing it through the legs with your other hand. Then practice by

taking short swings in front of the groin and catching the sticks with the hand.

As you get better, you may take a slow and easy swing to the back and down between the legs catching it in front. Be sure not to snap the

sticks between the legs, and keep the catching hand open wide till you feel the sticks contact it.

Practice with both hands, and practice catching them from the front and from the back.

Blocks

The high or rising block: snap up the sticks together and do a standard rising block.

The two-handed down or groin block: snap down with both hands holding the nunchaku.

The square or body block. Used to catch the wrist.

The two-handed downward block demonstrated.

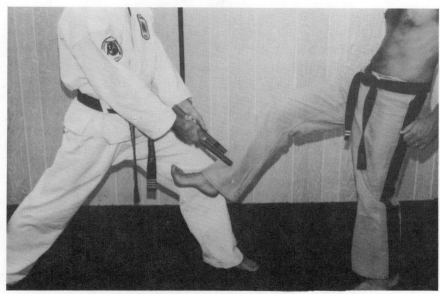

The leg block with the sticks spread in front.

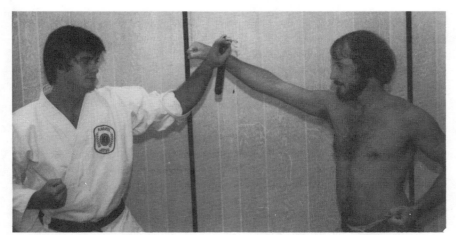

The rising block demonstrated.

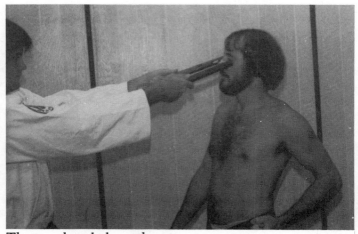

The two-handed eye thrust.

Striking Areas

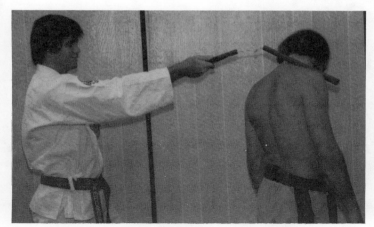

Strike the back of the neck and shoulders.

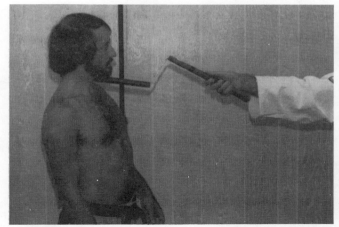

Strike the collarbone.

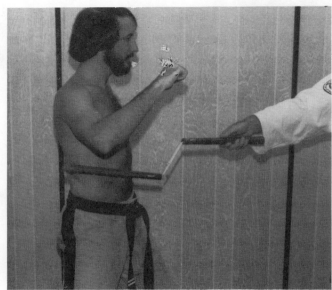

Strike the ribs.

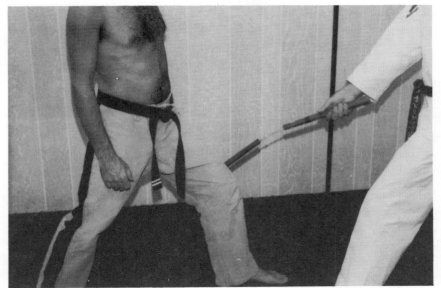

Smash the knee.

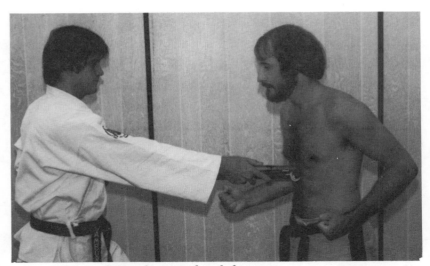

Thrust the sticks into the abdomen.

Slash the sticks across the face.

Wrist Lock with the Nunchaku

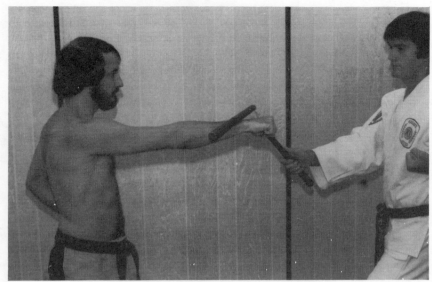

As he punches, flip the sticks up and over the
top of the wrist.

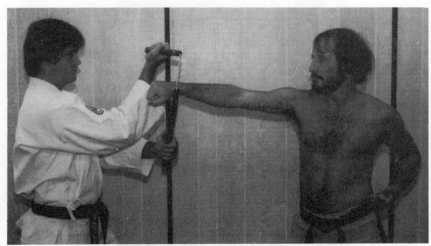

Now reach under and grab the end of the stick
and pull them close to the wrist.

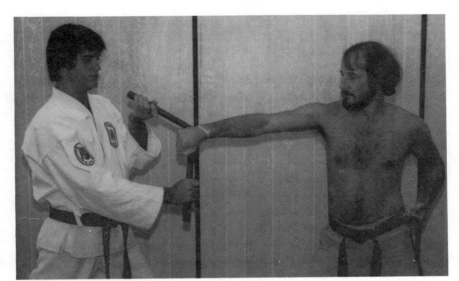

Wrap the sticks around the wrist very tightly.

Now squeeze and turn the ropes and grind them against the wrist, causing pain and controlling him.

Chokes

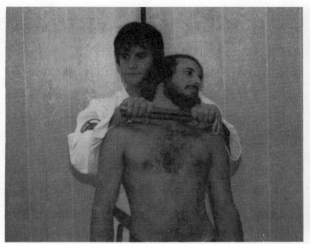

The two-handed straight choke behind the neck: lean his head back and hold the sticks on the ends and pull them against the throat.

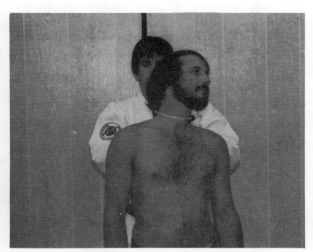

The string choke: wrap the sticks around the neck and squeeze them together choking him.

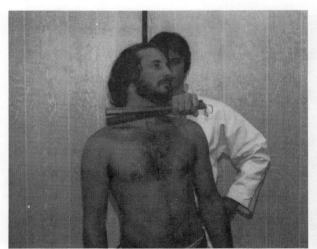

The X choke: this is the most powerful. Hold the sticks in the right hand and place them across the neck, now reach up with the left hand crossing your arms behind and grab the end of the

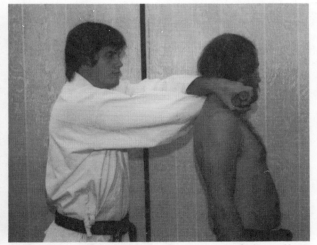

stick. Now lean back and squeeze while pulling down; this will choke him well and is very hard to get free from.

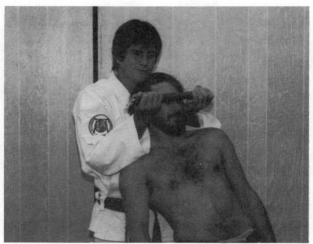

The eye and face smash from behind. You simply grasp the sticks in both hands and press them very hard against the bridge of the nose or mouth area.

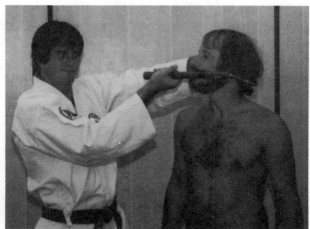

The face choke: wrap the sticks across the mouth and squeeze.

Techniques

A man attempts to strike at you. Ready the sticks in the behind-the-arm position, block his punch with your left hand, and smash the end of the sticks into his abdomen.

Come back with a flip smash to his collar bones;
then draw back your sticks for another strike as
he begins to fall over.

Smash the back of his head as he falls, and when he hits the ground smash the sticks into his back.

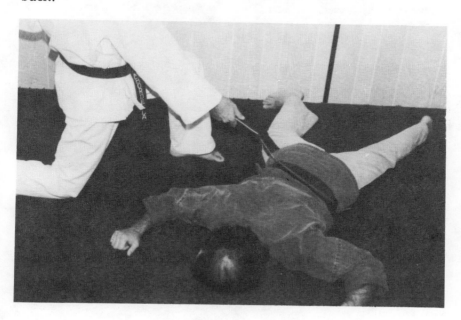

A man prepares to kick at you. You swing the sticks down onto his shin, breaking it.

Draw the sticks back up as he falls down from his broken shin.

Smash the back of his head.

Finish him with a string choke on the ground.

A man attempts to punch at you. You ready the stick behind the arm.

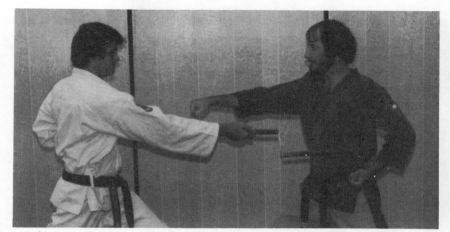

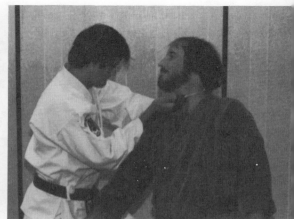

As he punches, smash the sticks into his ribs, then move to your left and wrap the sticks around his neck and give a quick hard jerk.

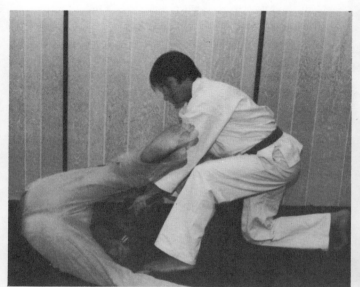

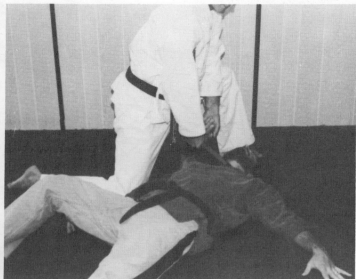

Throw him to the ground by pulling the sticks around his neck, and finish him there with a string choke by pulling the sticks together.

A man attempts to punch at you. You are ready with sticks behind your arm.

As he punches, swing a square block in front of you and this will catch his wrist and arm inside the strings of the sticks. Now quickly wrap the sticks around the arm and snap a roundhouse into his groin.

Step under his arm while tightening the sticks around his wrist. This will enable you to lock up his wrist and throw him to the ground, where you can finish him with a smash to the face.

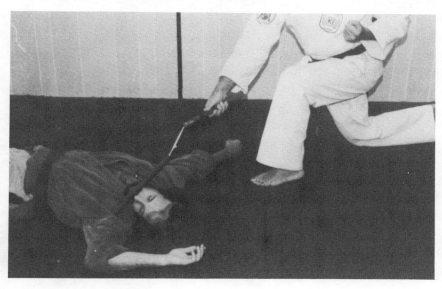

A man attempts to kick at you. Block down with a double-groin block and stop his leg.

Now drop your right stick very fast and wrap it around his foot, catching his foot in the string part of your sticks. This will lock his foot up, and by turning very hard in a circle you can throw him down to the ground.

On the ground, finish him by smashing the back of his head.

184

A man attempts to punch at you. Block up with a rising block with the sticks.

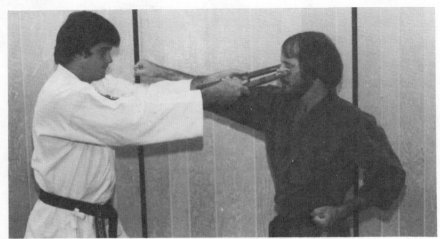

Now take both sticks and thrust the ends into his eyes.

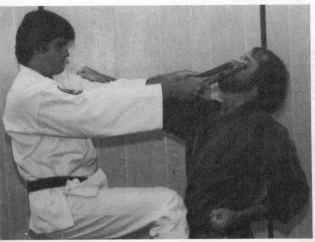

While poking his eyes, snap up a kick into his groin.

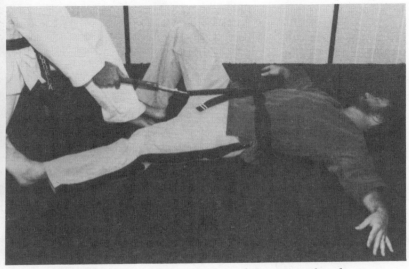

Finish him with a smash to his groin after he is on the ground.

Defense Against the Nunchaku

Wrap the gi top, or your coat, around your forearm and prepare to block using this as a target.

As he swings block up with a rising block with the gi top.

Now quickly, before he can move, smash a kick to his groin and a palm heel to his throat. This should knock him down.

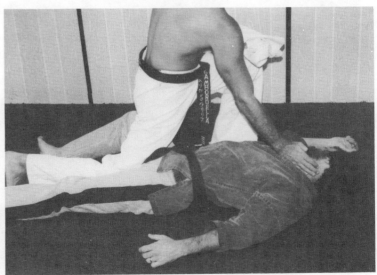

Finish him by a strong shuto to the throat.

Take off your belt and hold it extended between your arms, ready to block.

As he begins to move the sticks, flip the end of the belt into his eyes, blinding him.

Now before he can recover, smash a groin kick out.

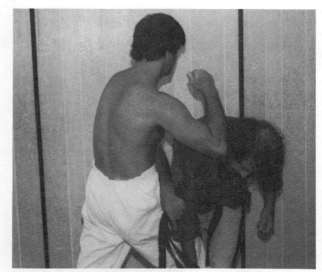

Finish him with an elbow smash to the side of the head.

Blocking the kick emptyhanded: prepare yourself to move very fast and with power.

As he starts his swing at you, jump out and hit his arm with a block with both your right arm and left hand.

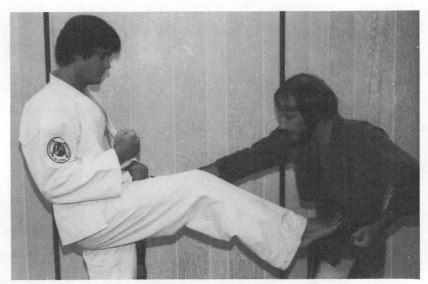

Now quickly step back and smash a kick to his groin.

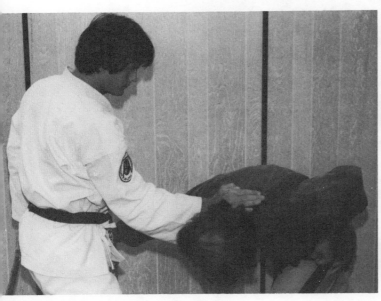

Finish him with a hard shuto to the back of his neck.

The following move requires intense concentration and speed.

As he swings the sticks at you, stay clear and watch the sticks intently, especially the string area.

Now flash out your hand between the swinging sticks and grab the string, stopping the sticks.

Continue to hold his arm and turn to your right
and smash an elbow into his ribs.

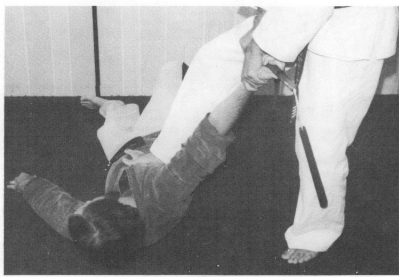

Throw him to the ground and finish him with a stomp to his
ribs, crushing them.

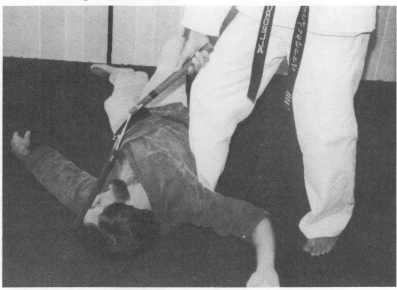

Then take his sticks and smash his head.

Blocking the Sticks
with the Jo

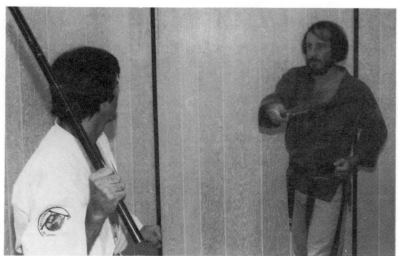

Hold the baton ready in your right hand as he comes at you with the sticks.

Now take the baton and thrust it between the sticks, catching them by the strings and intangling them, pull back sharply, and you will pull the sticks from his hands.

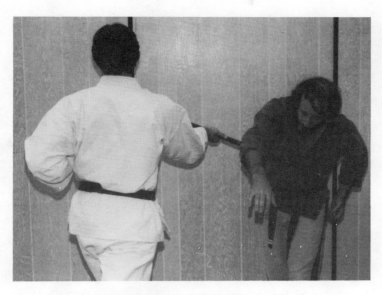

Counter with a smash into his ribs with the staff, and finish him by smashing the back of his head and neck.

Kata

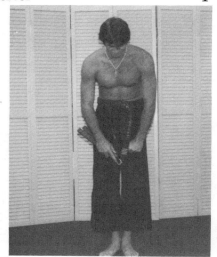

1

2

3

4

5

6

7

8

9

10

11

12

13

14

15

16

196

17

18

19

20

21

22

23

24

25

26

27

28

29

30

Chapter 7
The Sai

The sai is a weapon that has gained popularity in recent years because of its beauty in weapons kata and because of its practicality and effectiveness as a weapon of the martial arts. The sai was originally used to plant rice and is still in use in some parts of the world today.

It consists of a piece of steel or heavy metal that is approximately twelve inches in length, with a pointed or blunted end, and two prongs that extend down the blade to form a handle and a protection for strikes. All parts of the sai are used as a weapon—the end or butt for striking, the blade, the prong, and even the handle.

With a little practice, the sai can become one of the most beautiful and dangerous weapons you can learn to use. It is considered an illegal weapon in several states, so check with your law enforcement agency before carrying it on your person or in your car.

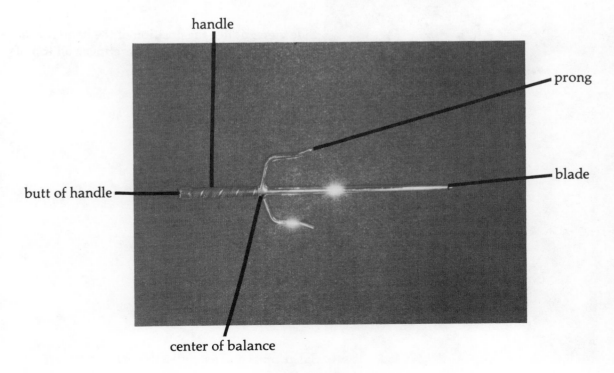

handle

prong

blade

butt of handle

center of balance

Holding the Sai

Blade down the arm: hold the handle of the sai with the forefinger wrapped around the prong, touching the thumb. The blade should extend down the forearm. Front view.

Side view: notice the position of the hand for the gripping. Fingers open with forefinger on top of the handle.

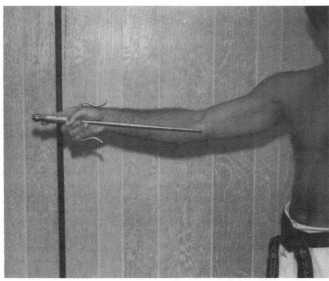

Sai gripped and extended down forearm.

Flipping the Sai

Starting position: holding the sai slightly pointed to the righthand side, begin to flip the wrist in a clockwise motion to the right.

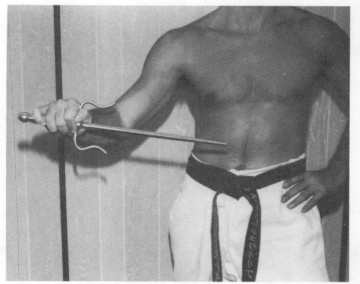

Middle of the flip: the blade is starting to come around and is supported by the thumb for leverage.

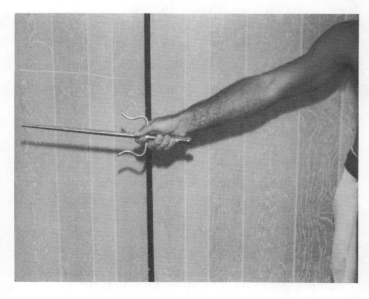

End of the flip: the blade is now in front, gripped with the thumb for control, and the forefinger is wrapped around the prong.

Close-up of Flips with Sai

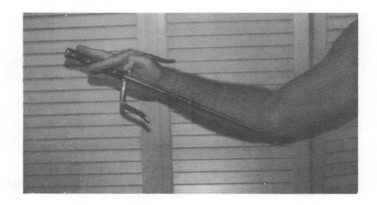

Sai being held down the arm, with three fingers wrapped around the handle and the forefinger down to the end of the handle.

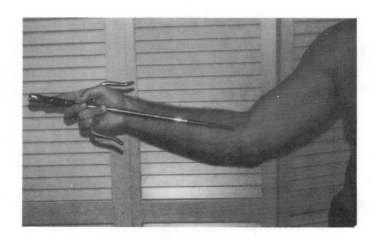

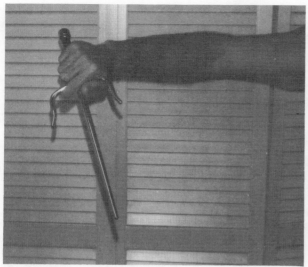

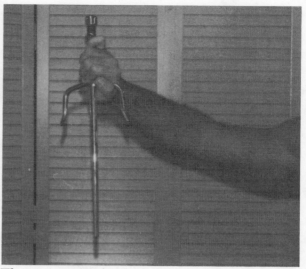

Lift all of the fingers and extend them down the handle to let the sai drop a little in your grip.

Then regrasp the handle with the last three fingers around the handle and the thumb near the prong.

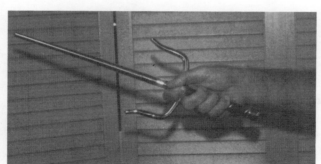

By now, the sai is horizontal and the wrist and fingers are facing away from the body; in other words, the wrist has turned completely around. Finish the flip by snapping the wrist back straight, and the sai will be pointed directly out in front of you. (Note: it is very difficult to learn to flip a sai from a photo, but if you try yourself and then refer to the photos, you will be able to master the flipping.)

Close-up of the Overhead Flip

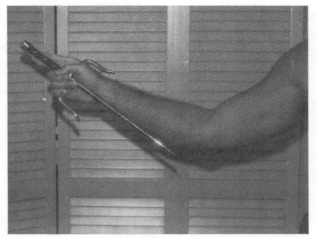

Begin with the sai held down the wrist. Now, slightly elevate the wrist and open the fingers so

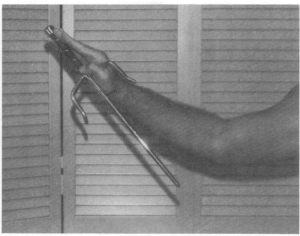

that the wrist may begin to move around the sai.

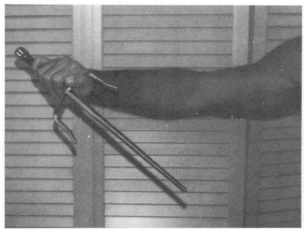

Grab the sai again. By now the fingers are around the front, and all are holding the sai.

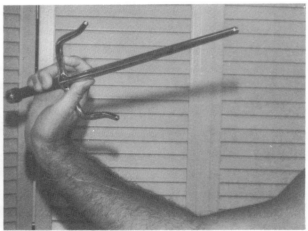

Lean the wrist backward and slightly open the fingers.

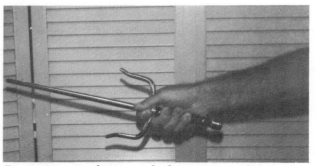

Begin to snap down with the wrist until the sai is pointed directly out in front.

The Sai Flip Demonstrated

An example of forward and overhead flips.

The left hand takes the sai and is flipping it forward.

Halfway through the move, the sai is cocked backward, and the fingers are down the blade ready to flip the sai.

To finish, the sai is held tightly again, straight out.

The right hand is flipping the sai for an overhead strike.

Halfway through the flip, the sai is pointed downward and the wrist is down with the fingers down the blade ready to flip the sai.

To finish, the sai is pointed outward and the grip is retightened.

Stances

Forward stance: the left hand has the sai down the forearm, and the right hand is up to protect and block the face. This stance is used for protection and defense from attack.

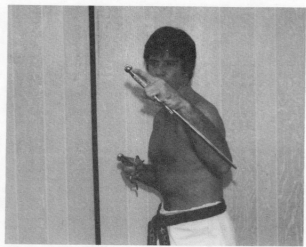

Cat stance: this stance uses the left-handed sai for blocking, and the right arm is back for punching.

Blocking cat stance: here the sai is drawn in the left hand and is ready to be used for blocking.

Natural stance: here, the feet are shoulder-width and both sai are across in front of the body ready for movement to block or strike.

Rising block.

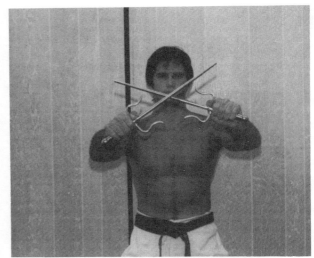

X block: used for knife and stick defenses.

Downward block stabbing: used to block kicks.

Forearm block: used for blocking punches.

Outer block, or wrist block: used for blocking staff attacks and kicks.

The X block for the groin.

The modified cat stance block for the side: this blocks the middle body and the face.

The cat block with the sai down the arm.

The face block with the thrusting sai.

Blocks

The lower block or groin block.

The middle block.

The side block or cat stance block.

The side lower block: used for blocking kicks.

Striking Positions
and Striking Areas

The sai can be used as would a knife or short stick. All areas of the sai are lethal—the blade, the heel, the prongs, and the handle.

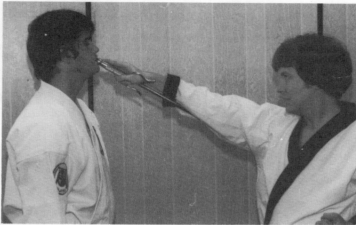

Driving the heel into the mouth: take the end of the sai and drive it into the mouth of the attacker.

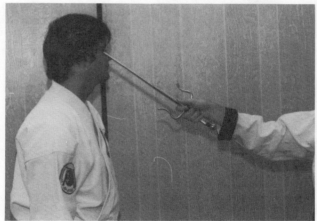

Driving the point into the eye.

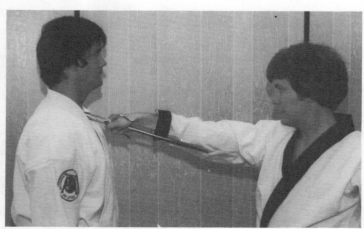

Driving the heel into the throat.

Driving the heel into the eye.

Driving the point into the abdomen.

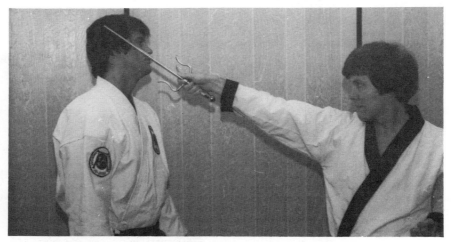

Striking the face with the blade.

Driving the point and blade into the groin.

Striking the groin with the heel.

Striking the solar plexus with the heel.

Backhanded strike of blade into abdomen.

Drive the point into the throat.

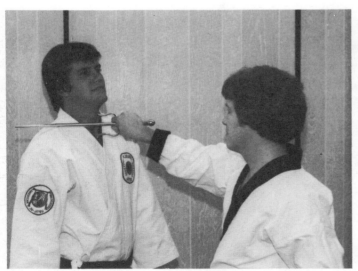

Drive the prong into the throat.

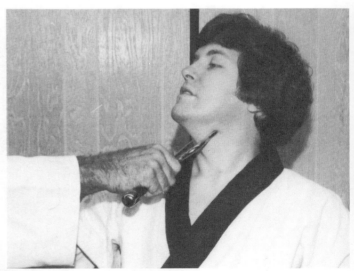

Close-up of prong striking neck.

Tearing the mouth with the prong.

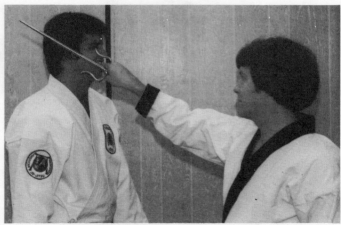

Driving the prong into the eye.

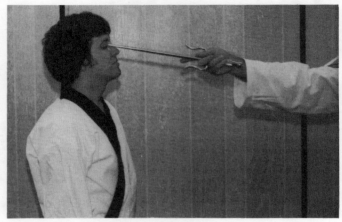

Driving the point into the eye.

Using the Sai
for a Wrist Control

The sai is very effective for controlling and
hurting the wrist. To do most wrist techniques
with the sai, simply grab the wrist between the
prong of the sai and the blade.

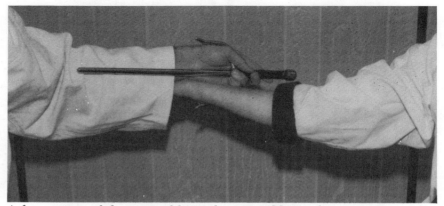

A front view of the sai grabbing the wrist. Note: the prong is under
the wrist, and the blade is across on top.

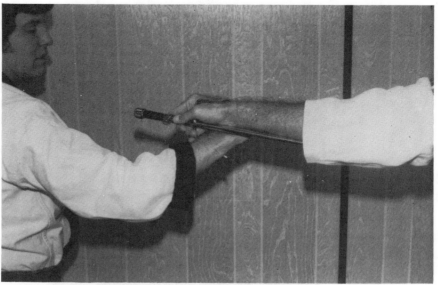

The back view of the sai grabbing the wrist. Notice the blade
pressing on the wrist bone for pain.

A block with the sai and a wrist lock being applied.

A rising block and a wrist lock being applied.

Techniques for Using the Sai for Defense

Ready for the punch.

Block the punch to the head with a rising block.

Counter with a strike to the eye with the heel of the right sai.

Follow up with a downward smash with the right sai into his groin.

This will cause him to lean over, and you can finish him with a stab to the back.

Ready to block the punch.

Block the punch by using a middle block with the left sai.

Counter by thrusting the right sai into his throat.

Finish him by smashing the right sai down into his groin.

Ready for the attack.

Block his punch with a middle block with the right sai.

Counter with a smash to the side of his head with the left sai.

Follow with a thrust of the heel of the right sai into his ear.

Now grab his gi with both hands and begin to throw him to the ground.

As he starts to fall, finish him with a stab to the throat with the right sai.

223

Ready for the strike.

Block the overhead strike with an X block.

Finish with a double thrust into the eyes of the opponent.

224

Ready for the kick.

Draw the righthand sai back for power to stop the kick.

Snap the sai down into the leg to break the shin.

Finish with a lefthand sai thrust into the abdomen.

225

Ready for kick: stand in normal position with both sai in front of body.

Block the snap kick with an X block.

Finish with a righthand sai smash into the face.

Ready for the kick: holding the sai in a side stance.

Flip the left sai down into the shin to stop the kick and break the shin bone.

Finish him with a strike of the sai to the neck to smash his face.

Ready for the block.

Use the double sai block to stop the roundhouse kick.

Finish with a thrust of the sai into the kidneys of your opponent.

Close-ups of Sai Blocks to the Leg to Stop Kicks and Control the Leg

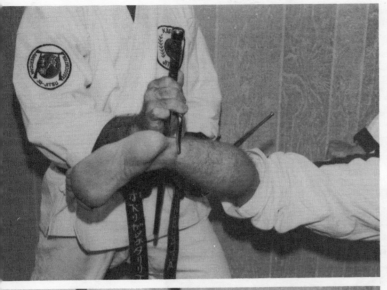

The front hook block: lock the leg by jamming the prong of the sai against the lower ankle. Lock the leg by jamming the sai against the shin and ankle.

Side hook block: block the kick by jamming the prong into the lower ankle, and follow up with a downward smash to the ankle bone with the other sai.

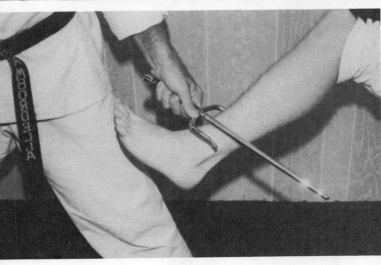

Block the front snap by jamming the prong down into the lower ankle part of the foot area.

Using the Sai to Stop an Attack from a Bo

Prepare to block the strike with the bo.

Block his overhead strike with a rising block with the right sai.

230

Counter by thrusting the left sai into his eye.

Unarmed Sai Defense

Ready to block the sai attack.

Use the X block to stop an attack to the face.

Continue to pull the right arm down and across the body, holding the wrist of the attacker to prevent escape. Follow up with a snap kick to the abdomen.

Ready to block.

Block his strike with the right sai with a rising block with your left arm.

Block his strike with the left sai with a right pressing block. Counter with a snap kick to his groin.

Step behind his right leg and throw him to the ground, where you finish him with a stomp to the throat.

Ready for the attack: block his strike with a rising block with the left arm.

Block his counter with the right sai by using a crossing block with the right hand. Counter him with a swift and strong groin kick.

 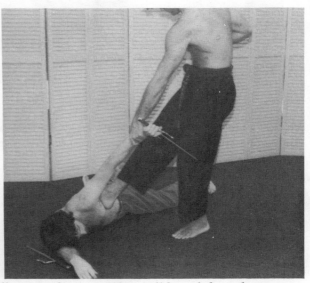

Now step into him and smash his abdomen with an elbow to the rear. This will knock him down, where you finish him with a stomp to the ribs.

Ready to block the attack.

Block his right sai with a rising block with the left arm. Now step into him and strike his throat with a right palm heel strike.

234

Grab his body and throw him over your hip to
the ground, where you finish him with a strong
shuto to the throat.

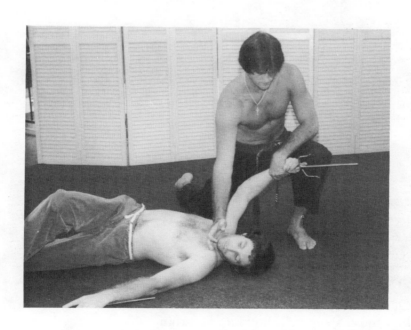

Ready to block his eye thrust with both sai.

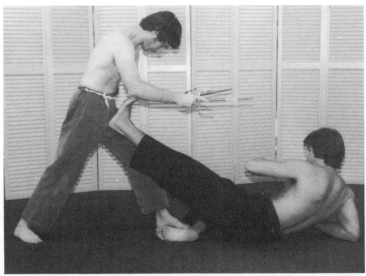

Quickly drop to the ground directly underneath
him and snap up your foot into his groin.

Defenses Against a Sai Using a Staff

Ready position: hold the staff down the right side.

Block the sai strike to the eyes with the staff, using an overhead smash to hit the sai with the staff.

Continue staff movement and strike back of his neck with the staff to finish him.

Ready for attack: staff held down right side.

Block the sai with a double-handed block.

Continue to move the staff and strike into the abdomen while holding the sai away from the body with the left hand.

Follow up with a strike on the back of the neck to finish your opponent.

Ready for attack: staff held down right leg.

Block the strike with the staff using an overhead smash.

Continue to move the staff in a downward circle
and strike the knee of your opponent.

Come back up and strike into the abdomen and
smash the ribs.

Finish with a snap kick to the head.

Kata